Haiku God

Study Companion

by

Stacey L. Jacobs, DMin

First Edition

© 2025 by Stacey L. Jacobs. All rights reserved. Fair use of this material is allowable for critical reviews, articles, local church teaching, or academic purposes. Else, no part of this book in any form may be reproduced without the permission of Stacey L. Jacobs.

Stacey L. Jacobs, DMin
Graphe1968@gmail.com

*Before the mountains were brought forth,
Or ever You had formed the earth and the world,
Even from everlasting to everlasting, You are God.*

- Psalm 90:2

TABLE OF CONTENTS

Preface 2
Theology Proper 5
Aseity 14
Beauty 18
Eternal 23
Immaterial 27
Immense 30
Immortal 34
Impassible 38
Immutable 43
Ineffable 49
Infinite 54
Life 60
Light 64
Majesty 68
Necessity 72
Omnipotent 76
Omniscient 81
Pure Act / Existence 87
Simple 91
Trinity 97
Unity 102
Wisdom 105
Omnipresent 108
Immanent 111

Transcendent	114
Sovereign	117
Love	120
Holy	123
Omnibenevolent	127
Truthfulness	129
Perfection	133
Jealousy	138
Justice	141
Wrath	144
Mercy	149
Anthropology	153
Bibliology	157
Hamartiology	162
Christology	167
Soteriology	171
Pneumatology	175
Ecclesiology	179
Angelology	183
Demonolgy	187
Eschatology	191
Acknowledgements	197

PREFACE

This book is written as a companion to *Haiku God: Some Mindful Musings on God, Creation, and Other Things*. Although *Haiku God* stands by itself as a substantive introductory Systematic Theology, *Companion* essentially offers the foundational philosophical and theological principles upon which *Haiku God* was built. For each topic, *Companion* includes the following:

- Topic Name
- Detailed Description
- Simple (but substantive) Supporting Arguments
- Supporting Scripture References
- Objections and Responses
- Practical Points to Ponder

The intent of *Companion* is to send the reader to a more contemplative and focused level of study, either during or after reading *Haiku God*. *Companion's* content is intended to be accessible to the reader, hopefully with concepts that have been reasonably simplified, but have not been made unduly simplistic.

The two works combined should be more than sufficient for any individual who is interested in further exploring the existence, attributes and characteristics of the monotheistic God of the Holy Bible—meaning reputable translations of the Protestant Bible in the context of this book—as well as some important aspects of the

Preface

cosmos that same God created. If more information is needed or desired, I then submit that perhaps a divine calling is upon one's life, and that person should probably consider—and would likely be best served by—finding a good institution of higher learning through which pursuit of these worthwhile ideas can earnestly continue.

Blessings and peace.

THEOLOGY PROPER

DEFINITION

Theology Proper is the study of the existence, attributes, and characteristics of God.

DESCRIPTION

This study is about *what* God is by Himself, and *how* God relates to creation. This includes God's moral and nonmoral attributes and characteristics.

An *attribute* is what God is within Himself. A *characteristic* is how God relates to creation. *Non-moral* means that God does not share a particular attribute or characteristic with creation. *Moral* means that God does, in some sense, share an attribute or characteristic with creation.

Pure Existence, Self-Existence, Infinitude, and Omnipotence are some of God's non-moral attributes. Clearly, these do not apply to the creation, including ourselves. We observe shortness of, decay within, and then cessation of life—both in and of ourselves as biological beings—with no inherent power to avoid any of those existential obstacles. We are finite beings who are dependent upon God for our existence. In that regard, our human nature is the opposite of God's nature, i.e., changing vs. unchanging; dependent vs. independent; mortal vs. immortal, etc.

God's non-moral characteristics are Omnipresence, Immanence, Sovereignty, and Transcendence. They show what God is within Himself and does not share with creation. All of these essentially show that God's rule and authority are equally present throughout creation.

Among His moral attributes, God shares Truth, Justice, Holiness, and Goodness with creation, particularly human beings. God's Mercy and Wrath are deemed moral characteristics, since there would be no need for either if there were no moral beings—whether physical or non-physical—to whom they could be directed, and to whom they could apply.

ARGUMENTS

All dependent entities need a cause.
The cosmos is a dependent entity.
Therefore, the cosmos needs a cause.

Nothing cannot produce something.
Only an existing something or someone can produce anyone or anything.
Therefore, the thing produced necessarily comes from a preexistent someone or something else, and its existence is dependent upon that preexistent someone or something else.

God is the Uncaused Creator of every contingent entity.
There is no contingent entity that does not have its origin from what God created.
Therefore, every contingent entity originates with God.

Either the universe has a beginning or it does not.
It is not the case that the universe does not have a beginning.
Thus, the universe has a beginning.

If the universe has a beginning, then it has a Beginner.
The universe has a beginning.
Therefore, the universe has a Beginner.

If there is no God, then all "god-talk" is nonsense.
All "god-talk" is not nonsense. If it were, then even talk about "there is no God" would be self-defeating non-sense.
Therefore, it is not the case that there is no God.

If there is no God, then science can explain all we need to know about anything.
But science does not explain all we need to know about (any- or) everything.
Therefore, it is not the case that there is no God.

Since the universe has a beginning, either a cause greater than the universe caused it, or something within the universe caused it.
Since self-causality is impossible, the universe must have a cause greater than itself.
Thus, the cause of the universe is greater than the universe itself.

Either an Uncaused First Cause created the universe, or the universe is eternal.
The universe is not eternal.
Thus, an Uncaused First Cause created the universe.

SCRIPTURES

Genesis 1:1-2—In the beginning God created the heavens and the earth. The earth was without form, and void; and darkness was on the face of the deep. And the Spirit of God was hovering over the face of the waters.

Job 26:7—He stretches out the north over empty space; He hangs the earth on nothing.'

Psalm 8:3-8—3 When I consider Your heavens, the work of Your fingers, The moon and the stars, which You have ordained, 4 What is man that You are mindful of him, And the son of man that You visit him? 5 For You have made him a little lower than the angels, And You have crowned him with glory and honor. 6 You have made him to have dominion over the works of Your hands; You have put all things under his feet, 7 All sheep and oxen—Even the beasts of the field, 8 The birds of the air, And the fish of the sea That pass through the paths of the seas.

John 1:1-5—1 In the beginning was the Word, and the Word was with God, and the Word was God. 2 He was in the beginning with God. 3 All things were made through Him, and without Him nothing was made that was made. 4 In Him was life, and the life was the light of men. 5 And the light shines in the darkness, and the darkness did not comprehend it.

Acts 17:25-28—25 Nor is He worshiped with men's hands, as though He needed anything, since He gives to all life, breath, and all things. 26 And He has made from one blood every nation of men to dwell on all the face of the earth, and has determined their preappointed times and the boundaries of their dwellings, 27 so that they should seek the Lord, in the hope that they might grope for Him and find Him, though He is not far from each one of us; 28 for in Him we live and move and have our being, as also some of your own poets have said, 'For we are also His offspring.'

OBJECTIONS & RESPONSES

Objection 1: There is no God.

God does not exist. God is a fiction created by people with frail minds so that their lives will have meaning, or they will have false comfort in dealing with the vast and grave difficulties that come upon them in life. There is no proof that God exists, and if God did exist, then he must not be a very good God because he allows evil to continue in this world. If God is so good, then evil and suffering would not exist. But evil and suffering do exist, and both to an unimaginably great degree. Therefore, God does not exist.

And even if God did exist, then he must be impotent—*powerless* to do anything about evil and suffering—or is malevolent, and thus unconcerned about evil and suffering. Besides, if God exists, then he should have created a world or universe where sin, evil, death, and other "bad" things are not possible. Yet, all of those things, and more, exist in the universe, so there must be no God.

Response 1: God does exist.

All dependent things need a cause. There are dependent things in the universe (at least I am). Therefore, I need a cause.

Now, some may argue that my parents are my cause. And that their parents are their cause. And so on. However, does this "line of parents" go infinitely backwards? Absolutely not.

Something does not come from nothing or no one. Someone or something must be the cause of something or someone. And that causal "someone" or "something" must itself be uncaused, for there is no such thing as an infinite regress of causality.

In that sense alone, there must be an Uncaused, and thus Self-Existent, First Cause of dependent things. And that is God. God alone is the Creator and Sustainer of the entire universe, down to the smallest existing atomic entity. God has made the universe as perfect as it could be made in its current form.

Sin and evil are committed by human beings. Much of the suffering in this world is caused by humans, which is the result—in a biblical sense—of the Fall from grace due to the choices made by humanity's biological progenitors, Adam and Eve.

Because humans can change and be changed, God's love and mercy offer a chance for them to morally change from evil to good; darkness to light; and rebellious to redeemed (see "Hamartiology" and "Soteriology," respectively).

Where evil and sin exist, God will one day eradicate both. But until then, God's great love and mercy for the universe He made—and especially the human beings made in His image and after His likeness—keep His wrath from destroying those who commit sin and evil. God wants none to perish because of sin, but for all to repent from it.

Objection 2: God cannot be known.

If it is true, as some "God-believing" people say, that God is infinite, eternal, transcendent, and especially, "incomprehensible," then it is clear that God cannot be known by anyone other than himself. Since we humans are finite, how can we comprehend what is infinite? Since humans are bound by time, how can we comprehend what is timeless? Since we are bound to a place in space, how can we comprehend what completely transcends time and space? Since words do not really capture the essence of anything, then how can our thoughts about God, as communicated through words, capture the essence of a God who is greater than words? Thus, God cannot really be known.

Response 2: God can be known.

To say that God cannot be known is to actually affirm that something about God can be known, i.e., that God is, in fact, unknowable. In that is the affirmation that 1) God exists, and 2) since God exists, at least one thing about God is knowable. Supposed self-referential, circular reasoning, and alleged semantics aside, there are other good reasons to believe that God can be known.

For one, God can be known *analgogically* and indirectly by what has been made, as seen with our own eyes, and as also contained in Romans 1:18-20. And while it is true that finite human beings cannot *comprehend* (i.e., have complete knowledge of) the infinite, eternal, transcendent, and "word-defying" God, we can *apprehend* (i.e., have some significant knowledge) things about God. Clearly, *complete* knowledge does not preclude *some* knowledge. When we observe change in ourselves and the universe; or see design that we create or observe; when we love or show mercy; or see the beginning or ending of life; we know that those things did not originate with us. In themselves, they provide evidence of one greater than us, and that one is God.

Also, our words do not have to have a 1:1, or *univocal*, relationship to what they describe in order to know something about the thing to which they refer. Just like "car" does not tell us every single thing about the construction, design, or operation of an automobile, the word "car" is yet understood by us to at least mean a single mechanical vehicular mode of transportation. So it is with words that talk about God: they do not capture the totality of His divine nature, but they are sufficient—because God made them so—to let us know that God exists, and that He loves us and is trustworthy.

Objection 3: The universe does not need a creator.

If God can be eternal, so can the universe. Many "God-believing" people say that God is uncreated and uncaused. So, if God does not need a creator and can be uncaused, then so can the universe. At least the universe is real and tangible; we are a part of it and are able to observe it. But God is invisible and cannot be observed by us. Would you not rather trust what can be observed and tested than a God who can neither be seen, touched, or felt? The universe was here before any of us were. And God only came into existence after humans got here because humans made up God. So, the universe does not need a "creator God" in order to exist. But God needs people in the universe in order for him to exist.

Response 3: The universe needs, and has, a Creator.

Simply put, the universe has a beginning. Even atheistic scientists hold to this demonstrable, scientifically observed, true fact. And since the universe has a beginning, 1) it is not self-existent, 2) it is a dependent entity, 3) it is not eternal, and 4) it needs a cause.

Since all dependent entities need an Uncaused, Self-Existent First Cause, that means the universe does, too. And that cause is God, as further delineated in Response 1.

PRACTICAL POINTS TO PONDER

1. People in this current age are becoming more and more secular as they ignore the clear evidence of God's existence. This is making

people in the world less respectful and loving to each other, and more likely to cause hurt and harm, both physically and spiritually, to one another. But giving good answers about the existence of God can help fight against this.

2. Understanding that God exists and can be known helps to build your own personal faith, and gives you the confidence to share your faith with others. Such a faith can change lives because it is logical, factual, reasonable, and true.

3. Knowing *what* God is helps you better understand *who* God is. Understanding "what" a thing is determines our attitudes about, and interactions with that thing. Because of "what" a dog is, we do not expect it to fix our computers or cars, pay our bills, or—reasonably speaking—answer our questions about the "deep things" of life . . . or even our prayers. Though other meaningful relationship is possible with canine companions, it is clearly not of the same quality, type, or category as human relationships. But because God is the Infinite, Eternal, Self-Existent, Unchanging, All-Knowing, Loving, and Merciful Creator of the universe, we know that we can interact in a meaningful way with Him about all things great and small. And because of "who" God is, we can trust Him to not only *hear* us, but also to *help* us.

ASEITY

DEFINITION

God is uncreated and Self-Existent.

DESCRIPTION

Aseity means "existing in and of oneself," or Self-Existent. It is important to note what Self-Existent does *not* mean, and then what it *does* mean.

Self-Existent does *not* mean that:
- God is *self-caused*. A self-caused being is a contradiction. A thing cannot be both its own cause and its own resulting effect at the same time and in the same sense. One must first *be* before one can *do*. God is not *self*-caused; God is *uncaused*.
- God needs a cause. This is based on a mistaken idea that since everything needs a cause, so does God. However, only *finite* (limited, contingent) things, i.e, things with a beginning, need a cause. God does not have a beginning. God is the Uncaused Causer and Sole Beginner of all—people, angels, animals, worlds, seasons, times, etc.

Self-Existent *does* mean that:
- God is Independent, i.e., needs nothing from anyone or anything in order to exist.
- God is the Uncaused First Cause of all things; there is nothing on which, nor anyone upon whom, God depends for "isness."
- God is not subject to anything or anyone outside of Himself in order to exercise His will, power, purpose or plan in the universe, even within our lives.

ARGUMENTS

Pure Existence has no cause.
What has no cause is self-existent.
Therefore, Pure Existence is Self-Existence.

God is Pure Existence.
Pure Existence has no limits.
So, if God was caused, that would be a limit to God's existence.
God has no limiting cause.
Thus, God is Pure (Self-) Existence.

God is Self-Existent.
Self-Existent is Independent of all else for its existence.
Therefore, God is Independent.

God is Pure Existence.
Pure Existence is uncaused.
Therefore, God is Uncaused.

If God is not Independent, then God was created.
God was not created.
Thus, God is Independent.

If God is Pure Being, then God is uncaused.
God is Pure Being.
Therefore, God is Uncaused.

If God is self-caused, then God cannot exist.
But it is not the case that God does not exist, for much evidence points to the fact that God does exist.
Thus, God is not self-caused. In fact, God is Uncaused.

Either God is Uncaused, Self-Caused, or non-existent.
God is not self-caused, for that is a logical and ontological contradiction.
God is not non-existent, for every dependent entity needs a cause, which itself cannot and does not need a cause for its existence.
Therefore, God is Uncaused.

SCRIPTURES

Psalm 90:2—Before the mountains were brought forth, Or ever You had formed the earth and the world, Even from everlasting to everlasting, You are God.

Psalm 93:2—Your throne is established from of old; You are from everlasting.

Acts 17:24-25—God, who made the world and everything in it, since He is Lord of heaven and earth, does not dwell in temples made with hands. Nor is He worshiped with men's hands, as though He needed anything, since He gives to all life, breath, and all things.

Revelation 1:8—"I am the Alpha and the Omega, the Beginning and the End," says the Lord, "who is and who was and who is to come, the Almighty."

Revelation 4:11—"You are worthy, O Lord, to receive glory and honor and power; For You created all things, And by Your will they exist and were created."

OBJECTIONS & RESPONSES

See those listed in "Theology Proper."

PRACTICAL POINTS TO PONDER

1. Contrary to popular belief, God does not need anything from us (e.g., our money, our time, our hearts, our souls, our praise, our worship, etc.) in order to be the Self-Existent God.

2. God's self-existence means that we can totally depend on Him for what we need, because He is always there for us, whether we *think* we need Him or not.

3. This should produce a profound sense of 1) *relief* that God is not depending on any of us; 2) *joy* knowing that our actions can not affect God's existence; and 3) *worship* of the True and Living God who exists all by Himself.

BEAUTY

DEFINITION

God is pleasing and admirable.

DESCRIPTION

When speaking of God in terms of *beauty* or being *beautiful*, one speaks regarding the foundation of aesthetics, i.e., pleasing appeal, which is essentially found in God. In a common sense, beauty is defined as the quality or aggregate of qualities in a person or thing that gives pleasure to the senses or pleasurably exalts the mind or spirit. It is to be generally pleasing; excellent (*Merriam Webster*). Likewise, it is loveliness, comeliness, fairness, prettiness, attractiveness, allurement, becoming, enthralling, or superior (*The Synonym Finder*).

Beauty includes, but also transcends, *physical* aesthetics, i.e., surface appearance or appeals to the five senses (seeing, hearing, tasting, touching, and smelling). Beauty is rooted in God. That is to say that the superior and surpassingly great existence of God means that He is the incomparable standard of what ultimately can please anyone or anything.

In this sense, God's beauty is said to have two aspects: *admirable* and *enjoyable* (Geisler, *Systematic, Vol. 2*, 244). *Admirable* beauty is objective, e.g., as found in a rainbow or selfless acts of kindness. *Enjoyable* beauty is subjective, e.g., one's love for vice or victory; the divine or debased; the lovely or licentious, no matter the cost.

The two together can be understood this way: God made the world objectively beautiful, but sin corrupted it. The world's beauty is still admirable, but sometimes not admirably enjoyed or enjoyable.

ARGUMENTS

To be beautiful is to be pleasing.
To be pleasing is to be able to meet an actual or perceived need.
God is Infinite, i.e., unlimited in essence and power.
Thus, God is able to meet all actual and perceived needs, i.e., is Beautiful.

To be beautiful is to be excellent or superior.
God is excellent in His existent and superior in His essence.
Therefore, God is beautiful.

Creation exhibits beauty.
But whatever is created exhibits the characteristics of its creator.
The creation comes from God.
Therefore, beauty comes from God.

If pleasing, then beautiful.
Pleasing.
Thus, Beautiful.

If God is not beautiful, then God is not admirable.
It is not the case that God is not admirable.
Thus, it is not the case that God is not beautiful.

If fellowship with God is enjoyable, then God is pleasing.
Fellowship with God is enjoyable.
Thus, God is pleasing.

Either pleasing or displeasing.
Not displeasing.
Therefore, pleasing.

Either God is admirable in His nature, or God is dishonorable in His nature.
God is not dishonorable in His nature.
Thus, God is admirable in His nature.

Either God has all ability to meet any actual morally holy need, or God is impotent in meeting such needs and thus displeasing.
God is not impotent.
God is not displeasing.
Therefore, God has all ability to meet any actual morally holy need.

SCRIPTURES

1 Chronicles 16:29—Give to the Lord the glory due His name; Bring an offering, and come before Him. Oh, worship the Lord in the beauty of holiness!

Psalm 27:4—One thing I have desired of the Lord, that will I seek: That I may dwell in the house of the Lord All the days of my life, To behold the beauty of the Lord, And to inquire in His temple.

Psalm 29:2—Give unto the Lord the glory due to His name; worship the Lord in the beauty of holiness.

Psalm 90:17—And let the beauty of the Lord our God be upon us, and establish the work of our hands for us; Yes, establish the work of our hands.

Psalm 96:4-6—4 For the Lord is great and greatly to be praised; He is to be feared above all gods. 5 For all the gods of the peoples are idols, But the Lord made the heavens. 6 Honor and majesty are before Him; Strength and beauty are in His sanctuary.

OBJECTIONS & RESPONSES

Objection 1: Beauty is in the "Eye of the Beholder"

Beauty is in the "eye of the beholder." This means that beauty in God is subject to how a person views God. What if someone thinks God is ugly? What if someone is blind? Therefore, God cannot be the source and standard of "beauty."

Response 1: Enjoyable beauty is subjective and sensory, while admirable beauty is immtuably aspirational.

A significant aspect of enjoyable beauty is about what a person perceives via sense perception (e.g., hearing, tasting, touching, smelling, seeing). This is necessarily subjective, as each individual may find different things sensorally enjoyable. God's beauty is admirable. It is the standard to which all beauty corresponds.

All admirable beauty is enjoyable, but some enjoyable beauty is not admirable. Some enjoy doing good things for other people, which is admirable, and pleases both God and others. On the contrary, some may enjoy doing evil things to others, but that is not admirable. God is displeased with things that bring undue and undeserved hurt and harm to others.

Enjoyable beauty is largely experienced via the senses and varies by each person. Admirable beauty is largely known, and done, via one's inner motivations for the good, which point back to God.

Objection 2: Beauty is about physical attributes.

The Bible says that "God is spirit" (John 4:24). Spirit is non-physical. Since beauty is about physical attributes, it is not possible for a non-physical being like God to be the source or standard for beauty.

Response 2: Beauty is more than physical attributes.

God is spirit, just as the Bible says, which would would logically be expected of a Self-Existent, Purely Existent, Infinite, Immutable, Eternal being. But like all words that intend to convey meaning, "beauty" is a reference to a transcendent reality. It thus finds its ultimate meaning in an unchanging, eternal source. Since finite things change in time, beauty does not find the locus of its meaning in them. God is the only unchanging, eternal being. Thus, "beauty," as such, finds its meaning in the immaterial, non-physical God, who is by nature, Spirit. Also see Response 1 for more insight about "enjoyable" versus "admirable" beauty.

PRACTICAL POINTS TO PONDER

1. God is to be praised and exalted because He is Beauty and altogether beautiful.
2. God is pleasing in and of Himself, so we should find our pleasure in worshipping God in the beauty of His holiness.
3. God is to be both admired and enjoyed for what He is in Himself, and who He is for us: Creator, Sovereign, Savior, Friend, and Lord.

ETERNAL

DEFINITION
God is timeless.

DESCRIPTION
Eternal is defined as having infinite duration, i.e., everlasting. It is for something or someone to be continued without intermission, i.e., perpetual. It is also to be timeless, always existing, endless, unending, never ending, continual, boundless, lasting, and enduring (*Merriam Webster*). Eternal does not mean "beginning-less time," neither does it mean "endless time." Eternality is "timelessness," i.e., non-temporal and not in time, but *beyond* time. To be truly eternal is to be non-physical (i.e., measureless, infinite, immaterial, etc.).

ARGUMENTS
God is Self-Existent.
Whatever is Self-Existent has no beginning in time, i.e., has always existed and is timeless.
Thus, God is Eternal.

God is Infinite Being.
Infinite being has no limits to its essence, e.g., time.
Thus, God is timeless, i.e., Eternal.

God is Immutable.
God cannot and does not change in essence or will, in time.
Thus, God is Eternal.

SCRIPTURES

Psalm 41:12-13—12 As for me, you uphold me in my integrity, and set me before Your face forever. 13 Blessed be the LORD God of Israel from everlasting to everlasting! Amen and Amen.

Psalm 90:2—Before the mountains were brought forth, or ever You had formed the earth and the world, even from everlasting to everlasting, You are God.

Psalm 103:17-18—17 But the mercy of the LORD is from everlasting to everlasting on those who fear Him, And His righteousness to children's children, 18 To such as keep His covenant, and to those who remember His commandments to do them.

Psalm 145:13—Your kingdom is an everlasting kingdom, and Your dominion endures throughout all generations.

Micah 5:2—But you, Bethlehem Ephrathah, you are little among the thousands of Judah, yet out of you shall come forth to Me the One to be Ruler in Israel, whose goings forth are from of old, from everlasting."

OBJECTIONS & RESPONSES

Objection 1: God Cannot Act in Time Unless He Exists in Time

God acts in time; whatever acts in time is temporal; thus, God is temporal.

Response 1: God is beyond time.

God acts *in* time but *from* eternity. He causes things *in* time from *beyond* time. He is the Beginner of all, yet has no beginning; the

Ender of all, yet has no end; the Sustainer of all, yet no need of sustenance; the Creator of all, yet uncreated.

Objection 2: Jesus Christ was Temporal, so God was temporal.

Jesus Christ was God; Jesus Christ was temporal; thus, God is temporal, i.e., exists in time.

Response 2: Jesus Christ has two natures.

Jesus is two "what's" in one "who." He is God the Son, who took on a body of flesh, and dwelt among humans (e.g., John 1:14). Jesus Christ was only temporal with respect to His human nature. In His divine nature as God the Son, who existed before the world was (John 17:5) and through whom all the worlds were made (John 1:1-2; Hebrews 1:2), He was Self-Existent and Infinite, meaning that Jesus' divine nature was not subject to space and time.

Thus, Jesus Christ was temporal in His *physical* nature, but is Eternal in His *divine* nature.

Objection 3: An Eternal God can have no beginning.

Everything that exists needs a beginning. God exists. Therefore, God has a beginning. Things begin in time. Since God has a beginning, God must have begun in time. These both mean that God is not timeless.

Response 3: God does not have a beginning.

Only *dependent* entities that exist need a beginning. God is Pure Being. God is Self-Existent. God is Independent in His existence. Therefore, God does not begin, nor has a beginning, in time. God created time and is beyond time. Also, dependent things need a timeless, independent cause for their existence. God is that timeless Uncaused being.

PRACTICAL POINTS TO PONDER

1. God's purpose and plan, which are identical to His nature, will not fail: to save humankind and reconcile to Himself those who have faith in Christ Jesus.
2. God's promises to us will come to pass: eternal life for those who accept Jesus Christ as Lord as Savior; the destruction of all evil; and bodily redemption of believers in Christ.
3. There is never a time when God is not with us, for He is timeless. Thus, God can always help us . . . any time . . . and always on time.

IMMATERIAL

DEFINITION

God is not made of, nor has any, atoms.

DESCRIPTION

Immaterial means "not of physical substance." In talking about God (practical theology), this signifies that God does not consist of matter, i.e., atoms, or atomic entities of any sort. Synonymously, it is incorporeal, discarnate, bodiless, unfleshly, impalpable, intangible, metaphysical, supernatural, and spiritual (*The Synonym Finder*). What this also means is that:
- God is not subject to decay or death.
- God is present to all space and time at the same time, without limit.
- God is not subject to any corruption or change in His being.
- God is Pure Spirit in His essential nature.

ARGUMENTS

A being that has no limits in its essence (Pure Actuality) can have no essential material parts.
Thus, God is Immaterial.

All matter is measurable.
But God is not made of matter and is thus immeasurable.
Therefore, God is Immaterial.

All matter exists in space and time.
God created, and is beyond, all space and time, i.e., Eternal.

Thus, God is not spatio-temporal, meaning God is Immaterial.

If unlimited, then Immaterial.
Unlimited.
Thus, Immaterial.

If God has no essential physicality, then God is Spirit.
God has no essential physicality.
Thus, God is Spirit.

If God is *made* of atoms, then God cannot be the *cause* of atoms (this is essentially self-causality, which is a contradiction).
God made all atoms.
Thus, God is not made *of* atoms (i.e., God is Immaterial).

Either physical or non-physical.
Not physical.
Therefore, non-physical.

Either God is a created being made of atoms, or God is an uncreated being with no atoms.
God is not a created being made of atoms, but the Creator of any being(s) made of atoms.
Therefore, God is an uncreated being with no atoms.

SCRIPTURES

Genesis 1:1-2—1 In the beginning God created the heavens and the earth. 2 The earth was without form, and void; and darkness was on the face of the deep. And the Spirit of God was hovering over the face of the waters.

Immaterial

Deuteronomy 4:15—"Take careful heed to yourselves, for you saw no form when the Lord spoke to you at Horeb out of the midst of the fire."

John 1:18—No one has seen God at any time. The only begotten Son, who is in the bosom of the Father, He has declared Him.

Colossians 1:15—He is the image of the invisible God, the firstborn over all creation.

1 Timothy 1:17—Now to the King eternal, immortal, invisible, to God who alone is wise, be honor and glory forever and ever. Amen.

OBJECTIONS & RESPONSES

See "Eternal, Response 2" re: Jesus' divine and physical nature.

PRACTICAL POINTS TO PONDER
1. God has no physical or time limitations.
2. God cannot be hindered in His divine will or actions by finite, physical, temporal things.
3. We should worship God in the way that is most like Him, i.e., in spirit and in truth (e.g., John 4:24).
4. We should live by faith and not by sight (i.e., 2 Corinthians 5:7).

IMMENSE

DEFINITION
God is immeasurable.

DESCRIPTION

Immense means "not measurable." It is defined as being marked by greatness, especially in size or degree. It is also transcending ordinary means of measurement (*Merriam Webster*). It also means vast, extensive, expansive, voluminous, capacious, massive, huge, enormous, large, big, staggering, stupendous, tremendous, titanic, colossal, humongous (*The Synonym Finder*), and ginormous. In addition, it means that:

- God is not limited by space.
- God is not limited by time.
- God is present at every point in space and moment of time.
- God interacts in time, but is not bound by it.

Immensity also implies that God has no physical presence in space or time, i.e., God has no materiality through which He occupies space and time; God does not need time in order to exist, nor to interact in the world. Because God is Immaterial, God cannot be measured by any means at all.

ARGUMENTS

A Being that has no limits in its essence (Pure Existence) is Immense (immeasurable).

An Eternal Being is unbounded by time, thus Immense (immeasurable).

An Immaterial Being cannot change because change involves a transformation of at least some "part" in time and space.
An Immaterial Being is also Eternal and has no physical parts in space nor time.
Thus, it is Immense.

Either limitless or limited.
Not limited.
Thus, limitless.

If limitless, then immeasurable.
Limitless.
Thus, immeasurable.

God is either measurable or immeasurable.
God is not measurable.
Thus, God is immeasurable.

If God is measurable, then God is not Infinite.
It is not the case that God is finite.
Thus, God is not measurable.

If God is measurable, then God is physical.
God is Immaterial and Eternal, neither of which is physical.
Thus, God is not measurable.

SCRIPTURES

Job 11:7-9—7 "Can you search out the deep things of God? Can you find out the limits of the Almighty? 8 They are higher than heaven—what can you do? Deeper than Sheol—what can you know? 9 Their measure is longer than the earth and broader than the sea.

Job 36:26—Behold, God is great, and we do not know Him; nor can the number of His years be discovered.

1 Kings 8:27—"But will God indeed dwell on the earth? Behold, heaven and the heaven of heavens cannot contain You. How much less this temple which I have built!

Isaiah 40:12—Who has measured the waters in the hollow of His hand, measured heaven with a span and calculated the dust of the earth in a measure? Weighed the mountains in scales and the hills in a balance?

Revelation 1:8—"I am the Alpha and the Omega, the Beginning and the End," says the Lord, "who is and who was and who is to come, the Almighty."

OBJECTIONS & RESPONSES

Objection 1: Jesus Christ was physical; therefore, God is measurable.

Jesus Christ was God; Jesus Christ was physical; thus, God is physical, i.e., exists in time.

Response 1: Jesus Christ has two natures.

Remember that Jesus is two "what's" in one "who." He is God the Son, who took on a body of flesh, and dwelt among humans (e.g.,

John 1:14). Jesus Christ was only physical with respect to His *human* nature. In His *divine* nature as God the Son, who existed before the world was (John 17:5) and through whom all the worlds were made (John 1:1-2; Hebrews 1:2), measurement was not possible because He is Immaterial, Infinite, and Eternal, none of which are measurable in time and space.

Thus, Jesus' *physical* attributes in His incarnation could be measured, but His divine attributes are immeasurable.

PRACTICAL POINTS TO PONDER
1. God's *love* is great and beyond all measure. There is always more than enough love for us all.
2. God's *mercy* is great and beyond all measure. God is always able to withhold justifiable punishment from us whenever we sin.
3. God's *grace* is great and beyond all measure. God is able to save us from our sins and sanctify any who believe in Jesus Christ at any time.

IMMORTAL

DEFINITION
God cannot decay or die.

DESCRIPTION
Immortal means "not decaying" or "undying." Immortal is defined as one exempt from death and oblivion: imperishable. It also means one that is not subject to decay (*Merriam Webster*). Similarly, it means deathlessness, athanasia, incorruptible, indestructible, everlastingness, unfading, amaranthine, never-ending, and unending existence (*The Synonym Finder*).

Immortal also indicates that God cannot be corrupted or corruptible in essence, i.e., become no more or less God at any time, neither can He be subject to moral or ethical actions that defy or deny Himself. God cannot cease to exist. God has always existed and always will exist.

ARGUMENTS
To be Immortal is to be Immutable (Unchanging).
God is Immutable.
Thus, God is Immortal.

Pure Existence cannot cease to exist.
God is Pure Existence.
Therefore, God cannot cease to exist.

Immortal

Death is a change from living to non-living, which occurs in time.
God is Eternal, i.e., timeless.
Thus, God cannot die, i.e., God is Immortal.

If dying, then mortal.
Dying.
Therefore, mortal.

If Immortal, then not decaying.
Immortal.
Thus, not decaying.

If God, then ever-living.
God.
Thus, ever-living.

Either God is Immortal or mortal.
God is not mortal.
Therefore, God is Immortal.

Either God is ever-living or God dies.
God cannot die.
Thus, God ever-living.

SCRIPTURES

Genesis 21:33—Then Abraham planted a tamarisk tree in Beersheba, and there called on the name of the Lord, the Everlasting God.

Psalm 102:25-27—25 Of old You laid the foundation of the earth, And the heavens are the work of Your hands. 26 They will perish, but You will endure; Yes, they will all grow old like a garment; Like a cloak You will change them, And they will be changed. 27 But You are the same, And Your years will have no end.

Romans 1:22-23—22 Professing to be wise, they became fools, 23 and changed the glory of the incorruptible God into an image made like corruptible man—and birds and four-footed animals and creeping things.

1 Timothy 1:17—Now to the King eternal, immortal, invisible, to God who alone is wise, be honor and glory forever and ever. Amen.

1 Timothy 6:15b-16—He who is the blessed and only Potentate, the King of kings and Lord of lords, 16 who alone has immortality, dwelling in unapproachable light, whom no man has seen or can see, to whom be honor and everlasting power. Amen.

OBJECTIONS & RESPONSES

Objection 1: Jesus is God. Jesus died, so God died.

Jesus Christ is God. Jesus Christ died. Thus, God also died.

Response 1: Jesus Christ has two natures.

Remember that Jesus is two "what's" in one "who." He is God the Son, who took on a body of flesh, and dwelt among humans (e.g., John 1:14). Jesus Christ was only physical with respect to His *human* nature. In His *divine* nature as God the Son, who existed before the world was (John 17:5) and through whom all the worlds were made (John 1:1-2; Hebrews 1:2), there was no possibility of death, because death involves change and the cessation of physical life, both of which occur in time; His divine nature is Immortal and Eternal. Thus, Jesus Christ died in His physical nature, but not in His divine nature.

This also lends great credence and insight to His claim in John 10:17-18 when He says "'Therefore My Father loves Me, because I lay down My life that I may take it again. 18 No one takes it from Me, but I lay it down of Myself. I have power to lay it down, and I have power to take it again. This command I have received from My Father.'" Through His *divine* nature, Jesus resurrected His *physical* body.

PRACTICAL POINTS TO PONDER
1. God is the Ever-living Creator of everything and everyone.
2. God is Incorruptible and is unaffected by malevolent and mean-spirited machinations of mortal humankind.
3. The Incorruptible and Immortal God will one day give every corruptible and mortal human being who believes in Christ an incorruptible and immortal body, but give every corruptible and mortal human being who does not believe in Christ the eternal punishment that each one's corruption deserves.

IMPASSIBLE

DEFINITION

God does not have emotions like humans do.

DESCRIPTION

Impassible means "not suffering." It is also defined as incapable of suffering or of experiencing pain, and inaccessible to injury (*Merriam Webster*). Some synonyms are impassive, insensate, impervious, motionless, and passionless (*The Synonym Finder*). The previous definitions and synonyms would seem to indicate that God has no feelings or emotions at all. However, that is not true.

God has emotions, but not in the way that human beings do. God always feels good about the good and bad about the bad. His emotions, in that sense, are the same as His nature, i.e., Unchanging. God never feels bad about the good, or good about the bad. Thus, it is important to note the ways that God does and does not have emotions.

God does have emotions or feelings, but they accord with His divine nature. God acts from His all-knowing insight, expressing profound, unchanging love and mercy towards humankind. However, God does not long or yearn for anything in the creation, manipulating some in order to get what He desires, then becoming miserable when He does not get it. God's sole yearning is that none would perish and that all would come to repentance (2nd Peter 3: 9).

God has unchanging emotions about the creation and the various entities within it. Relative to the actions of free moral mortal agents (humans), God always feels good about the good, and bad about the bad.

ARGUMENTS

To physcially suffer is to be (negatively, injuriously) acted upon by an outside agent.
But God cannot (negatively or injuriously) be acted upon by an outside agent, for to be negatively or inuriously acted upon is to be physical; but God is Immaterial.
In fact, God is the one who acts (righteously, mercifully, and justly) upon all agents, all of whom are outside of Himself.
Therefore, God can not suffer, i.e., is Impassible.

God is Self-Existent.
To be Self-Existent is to act upon, not be acted upon.
Thus, God is Impassible.

God is a Necessary Being who lacks nothing for His existence.
To have existential passions is to lack something either necessary or desired for existence.
Thus, God is Impassible.

If Immaterial, then free from suffering.
Immaterial.
Thus, free from suffering.

If anyone or anything can make God suffer, then God must not be All-Powerful.
The Self-Existent God is All-Powerful, for all else is dependent on, and comes from, God.

Thus no one or nothing can make God suffer.

If God is emotionless, then God cannot be Merciful.
But God is Merciful.
Thus, God is not emotionless.

Either emotions or no emotions.
Not no emotions.
Thus, emotions.

Either God has feelings or God has existential passions.
God does not have existential passions, for such passions express a need or desire that is crucial to one's existence. Yet, God is Self-Existent and needs nothing in order to be God.
Thus, God has feelings (i.e., Mercy, Love, etc.).

Either Immaterial and unable to suffer by some other agency or not.
God is All-Powerful Spirit and cannot be subjected to suffering in any way by anyone or anything.
Thus, God is Immaterial and unable to suffer by any agency, i.e., God is Impassible.

SCRIPTURES

Job 22:2-3—2 "Can a man be profitable to God, though he who is wise may be profitable to himself? 3 Is it any pleasure to the Almighty that you are righteous? Or is it gain to Him that you make your ways blameless?

Job 35:6-7—6 If you sin, what do you accomplish against Him? Or, if your transgressions are multiplied, what do you do to Him? 7 If you are righteous, what do you give Him? Or what does He receive from your hand?

Ezekiel 18:23—23 Do I have any pleasure at all that the wicked should die?" says the Lord God, "and not that he should turn from his ways and live?

Ezekiel 18:32—32 For I have no pleasure in the death of one who dies," says the Lord God. "Therefore turn and live!

Acts 17:25—Nor is He worshiped with men's hands, as though He needed anything, since He gives to all life, breath, and all things.

OBJECTIONS & RESPONSES

Objection 1: Jesus is God. Jesus suffered, so God suffered.

Jesus Christ is God. Jesus Christ suffered both before (e.g., Lazarus' death; beatings, etc., by Herod and Pilate's authority) and during the crucifixion. Thus, God also suffered.

Response 1: Jesus Christ has two natures.

Remember that Jesus is two "what's" in one "who." He is God the Son, who took on a body of flesh, and dwelt among humans (e.g., John 1:14). Jesus Christ was only physical with respect to His *human* nature. His *divine* nature as God the Son, who existed before the world was (John 17:5) and through whom all the worlds were made (John 1:1-2; Hebrews 1:2), is not subject to change in space and time, which suffering entails.

Thus, Jesus Christ suffered in His physical nature, but not in His divine nature.

PRACTICAL POINTS TO PONDER

1. God is not subject to manipulation in His feelings.
2. God is *trustworthy* since His feelings do not change on the basis of external agents.
3. God is *praiseworthy* because He does not vacillate in His feelings.

IMMUTABLE

DEFINITION

God is unchanging in His nature and being.

DESCRIPTION

Immutable means not able to change. It also indicates invariability, steady, constant, enduring, lasting, undecaying, incorruptible, and permanent (*The Synonym Finder*). This does not mean that God is unable to respond to us whenever there is a change in our life direction, mental disposition, or spiritual deportment. It does mean that God's response to our petitions and circumstances is in accord with His nature, i.e., He lovingly, mercifully, and consistently responds to sin, evil, repentance, and requests for forgiveness, etc., for our benefit but for His glory and honor.

Immutability entails the facts that neither God's essential nature nor will change. This is because:

God's *will* is identical to His unchanging *nature*.
God's *purpose* is identical to His *will*.
Therefore, neither God's *will* nor His *purpose* can change.

ARGUMENTS

God is Eternal.
Eternal means timeless.
Change happens in time, but God's essence is beyond time.
Therefore, God cannot change in His essence, i.e., God is Immutable.

God is Pure Being.
Pure Being necessarily has no potential to be anything other than what it is.
Whatever can be nothing other than what it is cannot change.
Therefore, God cannot change, i.e., God is Immutable.

God is Immaterial.
Immateriality has no atoms (physical parts) that are extended in space.
Physical parts can change. But if there are no physical parts, there can be no change.
Thus, God is Immutable.

If changing, then physical.
Not physical.
Therefore, unchanging.

If Eternal, then unchanging.
Eternal.
Therefore, unchanging.

If changing, then mortal.
Non-mortal.
Therefore, unchanging.

Either changing or unchanging.
Not changing.
Therefore, unchanging.

God either appears to change His mind, or God actually does change His mind.
God cannot actually change His mind, because change occurs in time (God is timeless), and God has no limit to His knowledge.
Thus, God only appears to change His mind.

Either God has emotions and is able to change them, or God is changeless in His emotions.
God has emotions, but does not exercise or "change" them in the way that humans do.
Thus, God has changeless (Immutable) emotions.

SCRIPTURES

Malachi 3:6—"For I am the Lord, I do not change; therefore you are not consumed, O sons of Jacob.

Numbers 23:19—God is not a man, that He should lie, nor a son of man, that He should repent. Has He said, and will He not do? Or has He spoken, and will He not make it good?

Psalm 102:25-27—25 Of old You laid the foundation of the earth, And the heavens are the work of Your hands. 26 They will perish, but You will endure; Yes, they will all grow old like a garment; Like a cloak You will change them, And they will be changed. 27 But You are the same, And Your years will have no end.

Hebrews 6:16-18—For men indeed swear by the greater, and an oath for confirmation is for them an end of all dispute. Thus God, determining to show more abundantly to the heirs of promise the immutability of His counsel, confirmed it by an oath, that by two immutable things, in which it is impossible for God to lie, we might have strong consolation, who have fled for refuge to lay hold of the hope set before us.

James 1:17—Every good gift and every perfect gift is from above, and comes down from the Father of lights, with whom there is no variation or shadow of turning.

OBJECTIONS & RESPONSES

Objection 1: God changes His mind in the Bible.

There are many instances where God changes His mind in the Bible. In Genesis 16:20-35, God threatens to kill all of the Israelites, but then only kills some of them. In Isaiah 38, God tells King Hezekiah that he is going to die, but then changes His mind and Hezekiah lives. This clearly shows that God is not unchanging.

Response 1: God only appears to change His mind.

While the accounts in Genesis and Isaiah seem to indicate that God changes His mind, it is not so. There is the appearance of God changing His mind.

Since God is Infinite and Self-Existent, there is no limit in God's essence at all, which includes His knowledge of everything at all times (Omniscience). In addition, God is Impassible, i.e., cannot be acted upon by the actions of anything outside Himself. God's essence does not and cannot change. Thus, God did not have to "change" His mind relative to the events of those passages.

However, it should be noted that God does have emotions and feelings, as demonstrated in His Love and Mercy. In each case, it could be easily and reasonably argued that God's Mercy and Love tempered His justifiable anger in Genesis, as well as His response to Hezekiah's sorrow in Isaiah. In each case, there was an opportunity for human repentance (i.e., a change in thinking) and the entry of

God's grace into their lives because of His great Love and Mercy. Even so, just because God responds to the human condition—as those conditions accord with His nature, i.e., sorrowful remorse and repentance—does not mean that God changes in His essence.

Objection 2: Jesus, who is God, died and was resurrected, meaning God changed.

Jesus Christ is God. Jesus Christ died during the crucifixion, then was alive again after the Resurrection. Jesus Christ changed, thus, God also changed.

Response 2: Jesus Christ has two natures.

Remember that Jesus is two "what's" in one "who." He is God the Son, who took on a body of flesh, and dwelt among humans (e.g., John 1:14). Jesus Christ died and was resurrected with respect to His human nature. His divine nature as God the Son, who existed before the world was (John 17:5) and through whom all the worlds were made (John 1:1-2; Hebrews 1:2), is not subject to change in space and time, which dying—and resurrecting—entails.

Thus, Jesus Christ died and was resurrected in His physical human nature, but not in His divine nature.

PRACTICAL POINTS TO PONDER
1. God's will does not change. His will is in accord with His nature. His nature is all-good and all-loving.
2. God's plan and purpose are identical to His will.
3. God's all-good, all-loving plan and purpose for our lives will never change.

4. This also means that we can have confidence, trust, and gratitude towards God, knowing that His plan of salvation—by grace, through faith in Jesus Christ—will never change.

INEFFABLE

DEFINITION

God cannot be comprehended, nor fully described, by words.

DESCRIPTION

Ineffable means not capable of being adequately expressed in words. Relative to God, it is simply saying that God's essence or essential nature—which is Eternal, Infinite, Immortal, etc.—cannot logically or otherwise be *fully* expressed via words, and thus not *totally* understood, i.e., *comprehended*, by anyone except God alone.

However, Ineffability does *not* mean there is absolutely *no* expression about God that allows us to know Him. God is not understood in a 1:1 (i.e., *univocal*) sense, which is impossible, since God is Infinite, and all "knowers" are finite. That is to say that God cannot be comprehended (i.e., in the fulness of His "isness") by anyone or anything that is not God.

Yet, it *does* mean that God can be understood *analogically*, i.e., a semblance of God's essence is able to be grasped by human understanding. It also means that knowledge about God can be *apprehended*, i.e., minutely, yet significantly, understood by human beings.

ARGUMENTS

God is Pure Being.
Pure Being is Self-Existent.
Self-Existent is Infinite.
Infinite is Immaterial.
Immaterial is Eternal and Immortal.
Eternal and Immortal are Immeasurable.
Immeasurable is Incomprehensible.
Thus, God is Incomprehensible.

If fully known, then comprehensible.
Incomprehensible.
Thus, not fully known.

If God is Infinite, then God cannot be fully comprehended.
God is Infinite.
Thus, God cannot be fully comprehended.

If someone has enough time, then God can be fully known.
But the Eternal, Immortal, and Immaterial God cannot be fully known.
Therefore, there will never be enough time to fully know God.

Either words are adequate to fully comprehend God or they are not.
But words are finite, while God is Infinite. Even the word "Infinite" does not and cannot encapsulate the actual "isness" of God's limitless existence.
Thus, words are not adequate to comprehend the "isness" of God.

God can be either comprehended or apprehended.
God cannot be comprehended.
Thus, God can be apprehended.

Ineffable

God is either fully knowable or unknowable.
God is not fully knowable.
Neither is God unknowable.
Thus, God must be knowable in some other way, which is partially knowable.

SCRIPTURES

Deuteronomy 29:29—The secret things belong to the LORD our God, but those things which are revealed belong to us and to our children forever, that we may do all the words of this law.

Job 11:7—Can you search out the deep things of God? Can you find out the limits of the Almighty?

Isaiah 55:8-9—8 " For My thoughts are not your thoughts, nor are your ways My ways," says the LORD. 9 " For as the heavens are higher than the earth, so are My ways higher than your ways, and My thoughts than your thoughts.

Romans 11:33—"Oh, the depth of the riches both of the wisdom and knowledge of God! How unsearchable are His judgments and His ways past finding out!"

Ephesians 3:20—Now to Him who is able to do exceedingly abundantly above all that we ask or think, according to the power that works in us

OBJECTIONS & RESPONSES

Objection 1: If God can be partially known, then maybe God can be fully known.

Partial knowledge of God's nature is possible, if only through what has been created, as Romans 1:18-20 says. Thus, it appears that the logical possibility exists for God to be fully known via the existing universe, if only there is enough time search it out. This appears to call into serious question the idea that God cannot be comprehended.

Response 1: It is logically and actually impossible to fully comprehend God.

God is Infinite Being. Any "knower" is finite being. That alone says that actual comprehension of God is logically impossible, for limited cannot "get to the end" of that which is unlimited—and thus immeasurable or even fully observable.

Still, since God is Infinite Being, there would also have to be an actual "infinite knower" besides God, who would not be able to merely "traverse" the actual infinite essence of God, but would actually be God in essence. That would also present the conundrum of two actual Infinite Beings. Both the "infinite knower" and the "other actual Infinite Being" are logical and actual impossibilities. Thus, God is, and will remain, Ineffable.

PRACTICAL POINTS TO PONDER

1. No one can "figure out" God.
2. No one should ever become so proud as to think one can never learn more about God. God is Infinite, Eternal, Immense, and Immortal. God will outlast, outlive, and is too great for any of us to comprehend.

3. Nearly anyone can *apprehend* the nature and existence of God, but no one can ever fully *comprehend* them.
4. Every effort should be taken to learn what can be known about God, then live by and give that knowledge to other people. God lives, loves, and saves to the uttermost.

INFINITE

DEFINITION
God has no limits to His essence or nature.

DESCRIPTION
Infinity means "not finite," i.e., unlimited. It is to be unimaginably great, to the extent that perfect, boundless, eternal existence is real and actual. This is God in His existence.

Infinity does *not* mean that:
- There is an actual infinite series of numbers.
- An infinite series of divisible space between two points.
- An actual infinite series of real things.
- "A gazillion-gajillion-bazillion-gadrillion-gadillion-badrillion-katillion to that power."

What Infinite *does* mean is that God's essential nature is not limited in any way (e.g., power, knowledge, existence, presence, love, mercy, etc.), and that there can be only one "Infinite Being." Infinite entails the notion of "all in its class." There is only one calss of "Uncaused Self-Existent First Causes," so there can never be two "alls" in that same class at the same time and in the same sense. Only God occupies that class, which puts God in class all by Himself. Thus, only God is truly Infinite.

ARGUMENTS
An Infinite Being is not bound by anything or anyone outside of itself.
Whatever is not bound by anyone or anything is without limit.
God is not bound by anyone or anything outside of Himself.

Infinite

Therefore, God is without limit, i.e., Infinite.

God is Self-Existent.
Self-Existent is Eternal and Immaterial.
Eternal and Immaterial are Immortal.
Immortal is Immeasurable.
Immeasurable is Immense.
Immense is Infinite.
Thus, God is Infinite.

If Immortal, then Infinite.
Immortal.
Thus, Infinite.

If God is infinite, which means "all" being, then all being is God.
If all being is God, then everything *is* God, meaning everything is really one singular being.
However, there are other *dependent* "beings" created by God whose essences and natures *differ* from God's.
Thus, though God is Infinite Being and the Source of dependent beings, God is not "all" being(s); all being is not God; and all being is not one singular being.

If God is Infinite, then the universe cannot "hold" Him.
God is Infinite.
Therefore, the universe cannot "hold" God, i.e., contain His essence.

Either mortal or Immortal.
Non-mortal.
Thus, Immortal.

Either Infinite and Immortal, or finite.
Not finite.
Therefore, Infinite and Immortal.

Either God is unlimited in Essence, or God can be controlled by some entity apart from Himself.
God, as Pure, Immortal Self-Existence cannot be controlled by anything apart from Himself.
Thus, God is unlimited Essence, i.e., Infinite.

SCRIPTURES

1 Kings 8:27—But will God indeed dwell on the earth? Behold, heaven and the heaven of heavens cannot contain You. How much less this temple which I have built!

Psalm 147:5—Great is our Lord, and mighty in power; His understanding is infinite.

Isaiah 41:4—Who has performed and done it, Calling the generations from the beginning? 'I, the Lord, am the first; And with the last I am He.' "

Isaiah 9:6-7—6 For unto us a Child is born, Unto us a Son is given; And the government will be upon His shoulder. And His name will be called Wonderful, Counselor, Mighty God, Everlasting Father, Prince of Peace. 7 Of the increase of His government and peace there will be no end.

Isaiah 46:9-10—9 Remember the former things of old, For I am God, and there is no other; I am God, and there is none like Me, 10 Declaring the end from the beginning, And from ancient times things that are not yet done, Saying, 'My counsel shall stand, And I will do all My pleasure.'

Revelation 1:8, 11, 18—8 "I am the Alpha and the Omega, the Beginning and the End," says the Lord, "who is and who was and who is to come, the Almighty"; 11 ". . . I am the Alpha and the Omega, the First and the Last . . ."; 18 "I am He who lives, and was dead, and behold, I am alive forevermore. Amen . . ."

OBJECTIONS & RESPONSES

Objection 1: If God is "all" being, then there is no "other" being.

God is infinite in being.
There cannot be more being than infinite being, because "infinite" means "all."
Therefore, there is really no other being except God, which would infer that God is all being, and all being is God.

Response 1: There is more than one type of "being" and / or existence.

First, "infinite" is *qualitative* and does not necessarily mean, *quantitatively*, "all." Infinite more accurately means "without limit" relative to the *quality* of an entity's existence, in this case, God's. Thus, it should also be noted that there are other *qualitative* "being" and "beings" besides God; the Self-Existent God actually made them.

For example, human beings—and other biological life—are finite in their nature, because they are space and time-bound mortals. Angels (and demons) are neither finite nor infinite, but *aeviternal*, i.e., created in time, but do not die or have an end to their existence

(Thomas, *Summa*). Inanimate objects are also finite in being and subject to decay. Thus, it is clear that there are other beings that exist, and their being and existence are in no way compromised by God's Infinite Being and (Self-) Existence.

Last, the idea that "all is God, and God is all" is called *pantheism*, literally "all is God," which leads to the state of monism, meaning that "all is one." This is contrary to *monotheism*, meaning only one God who created the universe and is still active in it.

If all is God, and God is all, and thus all is "one," then 1) there would be no "I" and "other than I"; and 2) it would be completely nonsensical to distinguish any one thing from another: a tree, car, rock, mucous, mite, money, manatee, or amoeba are all actually the same one thing. This is logical and theological nonsense.

Objection 2: Jesus, who is God, was not infinite.

Jesus Christ is God. According to the Bible, Jesus did not always exist on earth; he was born in time; grew up on earth; died; and was resurrected.
Jesus Christ not only changed, but showed limitations in his existence.
Thus, God is limited, i.e., not infinite.

Response 2: Jesus Christ has two natures.

Remember that Jesus is two "what's" in one "who." He is God the Son, who took on a body of flesh, and dwelt among humans (e.g., John 1:14). Jesus Christ was born, then grew up, died, and was resurrected with respect to His human nature. His divine nature as God the Son, who existed before the world was (John 17:5) and through whom all the worlds were made (John 1:1-2; Hebrews 1:2), is not subject to change in space and time, which His birth, growth, dying, resurrecting, et al, entail.

Thus, Jesus Christ was limited in His physical human nature, but not in His divine nature.

PRACTICAL POINTS TO PONDER
1. There is no limit or lack in God whatsoever. God is inexhaustible "isness."
2. God has every good and perfect thing, within Himself, that we can possibly need or desire (God is Beautiful!).
3. God has an infinite supply of love, mercy, compassion, kindness, wisdom, knowledge, power, etc., to meet every need of everyone and everything in the universe.

LIFE

DEFINITION

God is life and the source of life for all living entities.

DESCRIPTION

Because God is Purely Self-Existent and Immortal, it stands to reason that God is also *Life*. God's Life and Immortality are inseparably bound together. There is no significant difference between the two, yet the two are distinct.

Immortal means that God cannot decay or die. Immortality cannot be separated from Eternality. It thus reasonably and necessarily follows that Life, and that Eternal and Infinite, flows from Immortality. *Life* is more akin to the idea that God is always consciously, conscientiously, and actively controlling, ruling, and sustaining the universe. This is because, again, God is Pure Self-Existent Act. In other words, God is always simply "being" God, or simply "Godding." In that sense, God is the Uncaused Actual, Animating and Sustaining Source of all other life.

ARGUMENTS

God is Pure Self-Existent Act.
Pure Self-Existent Act is Infinite.
Infinite is Eternal.
Eternal is Immortal.
Immortal is Life.
Thus, God is Life.

Mortal entities are born, live, then die in space and time.

Life

Mortal entities must then ultimately need a non-mortal source for their existence, i.e., living, that is not subject to space and time.
God is not subject to space and time for His existence.
Thus, God must be the Source for the existence, i.e., life, of all mortal entities.

God is Life.
Life is a beautiful attribute of God.
God gave humans life.
Thus, God gave humans something beautiful.

God is Life and Life is beautiful.
If beautiful, then should be cherished.
Therefore, life should be cherished.

If God cannot die, then God is Immortal Life.
God cannot die.
Thus, God is Immortal Life.

If finite things live, then they must have an infinite source of Life.
Finite things live.
Therefore, finite things have an infinite source of life, i.e., God.

Either mortal or non-mortal.
Not mortal.
Thus, non-mortal.

Either God is the Source of Life or God is not the Source of Life.
It is not the case that God is not the Source of life.
Thus, God is the Source of Life.

Faith in Jesus Christ leads to Eternal Life or it does not lead to Eternal Life.
It is not true that faith in Jesus Christ does not lead to Eternal Life.
Thus, faith in Jesus Christ does lead to Eternal Life.

SCRIPTURES

Genesis 2:7—And the Lord God formed man of the dust of the ground, and breathed into his nostrils the breath of life; and man became a living being.

Job 33:4—The Spirit of God has made me, And the breath of the Almighty gives me life.

Psalm 42:8—The Lord will command His lovingkindness in the daytime, And in the night His song shall be with me—A prayer to the God of my life.

John 6:33—For the bread of God is He who comes down from heaven and gives life to the world.

John 14:6—Jesus said to him, "I am the way, the truth, and the life. No one comes to the Father except through Me.

OBJECTIONS & RESPONSES

Same as for "Immortality" re: Jesus.

PRACTICAL POINTS TO PONDER

1. God is the Unending Source of all life.
2. God is Incorruptible and is unaffected by the schemes, plans, whims, and will of mortal man.
3. The Incorruptible and Immortal God will one day give every corruptible and mortal man (who believes in Christ) an

Life

incorruptible and immortal body, with which they will then experience everlasting life.

LIGHT

DEFINITION

God is moral light.

DESCRIPTION

God is not physical light. Physical light is photons. God made physical light.

God is *spiritual* or *moral* light. God illuminates the minds of human beings so they can better understand things pertaining to life and godliness as they believe in Him.

Whenever the Bible speaks of God in the sense of "being" light, this is a figure of speech called *metaphor* (Zuck, *Bible*). This means that human writers use human words to compare non-human things. In this case, physical light is used to describe the non-human, non-physical God, who is the Creator of all humans and the entire cosmos.

In the Bible, spiritual leaders in the Old and New Testaments are sometimes called "blind" by God. This is not because they were physically blind and unable to detect photonic, electromagnetic energy with their actual eyes. It is because they were willingly ignoring or disobeying God's commands, both direct and revealed through His Word, and were thus considered "spiritually blind," i.e., unable to "see" God's "spiritual light."

God is Spiritual Light that illuminates the *moral* paths of *mortal* people.

Light

ARGUMENTS

God is non-temporal (Eternal) and non-spatial (Immaterial).
Electromagnetic light is both spatial and temporal.
Thus, God cannot be electromagnetic light.
But God has been called a "light" in the Bible.
God has also been called a "spirit" in the Bible.
Thus, God as a non-spatial, non-temporal spirit can be, and is, Spiritual Light.

If not physical, then spirit.
Not spirit.
Thus, physical.

If non-physical, then not physical light.
Non-physical.
Thus, not physical light.

Either the cause or the effect.
Not the effect.
Therefore, the cause.

If God created physical light, then God cannot be physical light.
God created physical light.
Thus, God cannot be physical light.

Either God causes physical light and is actual moral light, or God is actual physical light, or God is both the cause and effect of physical light.
God is not physical light, for God is Immaterial.
God is not the cause *of*, and the resulting effect that *is*, physical light; that is a logical and actual impossibility.

Thus, God is the Cause of physical light and is actual moral light.

SCRIPTURES

Genesis 1:3-4—Then God said, "Let there be light"; and there was light. And God saw the light, that it was good; and God divided the light from the darkness.

Isaiah 50:10—"Who among you fears the Lord? Who obeys the voice of His Servant? Who walks in darkness And has no light? Let him trust in the name of the Lord And rely upon his God."

Daniel 5:14—I have heard of you, that the Spirit of God is in you, and that light and understanding and excellent wisdom are found in you.

John 1:4-5—4 In Him was life, and the life was the light of men. 5 And the light shines in the darkness, and the darkness did not comprehend it.

John 3:19-21—19 And this is the condemnation, that the light has come into the world, and men loved darkness rather than light, because their deeds were evil. 20 For everyone practicing evil hates the light and does not come to the light, lest his deeds should be exposed. 21 But he who does the truth comes to the light, that his deeds may be clearly seen, that they have been done in God.

OBJECTIONS & RESPONSES

None noted. See also the above arguments in this section.

PRACTICAL POINTS TO PONDER

1. Spiritual blindness is the key problem that plagues our world today because people willingly ignore God's existence and God's prescriptive exhortations to love, repent, be saved, etc.

Light

2. God does not want humankind to remain "blind" to the truth of His love, mercy, and salvation.
3. God is (moral and spiritual) Light that helps guide our lives, according to His will and good pleasure, even as revealed in His Word, the Bible.

MAJESTY

DEFINITION

God is infinitely great and is without equal.

DESCRIPTION

When one hears the word "majesty," there is tremendous likelihood that images of kings, queens, princes, princesses, crowns, castles, and other accoutrements befitting the word come to mind. In addition, there are probably the related ideas of rule, sovereignty, authority, and headship. Those words are appropriate when considering that God is majestic, and *Majesty* is in His essential being.

Majestic is derived from the Latin word *major*, meaning "greater" (*Merriam Webster*). God is magnificent in His being. Nothing or no one exceeds God in magnficence. God's majesty is also evident via what the creation itself is, i.e., what it displays: the Beauty of God, and the innate knowledge of humankind that God lovingly and mercifully rules and has unfettered authority over all existence.

Thus, when considering alone the macrocosmic vastness and intricate microcosmic complexity of creation, it is apparent that God is not merely great, but the greatest Being there is . . . and His greatness is unsurpassed.

ARGUMENTS

God is Infinite Being.
Infinite Being is unlimited in Essence.
No other essence is, nor can be, greater than God's.
Therefore, no one or nothing is greater than God, i.e., God is Majestic.

To be finite and mortal is to be measurable in time and space.
To be infinite and immortal is to be immeasurable in time and space.
God is Infinite and Immortal.
Thus, God has no equal in time or space.

Infinity cannot be traversed or comprehended.
God is Infinite.
Thus, God cannot be traversed or comprehended, i.e., God is unsurpassable.

If great or greater, then not the greatest.
Great.
Therefore, not greatest.

If greatest, then unsurpassable.
Greatest.
Therefore, unsurpassable.

Either great is the ultimate state of being, or some other state of being is greater.
Great is not the ultimate state of being.
Thus, some other state of being is greater.

Either physical existence is the greatest type of existence, or some other type of existence is greater than physical existence.
Physical existence is not the greatest type of existence because physical existence decays and changes.
Therefore, some other type of existence is greater than physical existence.

Either temporal existence is the greatest type of existence, or some other type of existence is greater than temporal existence.
Temporal existence is not the greatest type of existence because temporal existence is limited and finite.
Therefore, some other type of existence is greater than physical existence.

Either God's Self-Existence is the ultimate existence, or some other type of existence is ultimate existence.
But there can be no other type of existence greater than Self-Existence.
Thus, God's Self-Existence is ultimate existence.

SCRIPTURES

1 Chronicles 16:26-27—26 For all the gods of the peoples are idols, But the LORD made the heavens. 27 Honor and majesty are before Him; Strength and gladness are in His place.

1 Chronicles 29:11—Yours, O LORD, is the greatness, The power and the glory, The victory and the majesty; For all that is in heaven and in earth is Yours; Yours is the kingdom, O LORD, And You are exalted as head over all.

Psalm 145:4-6—4 One generation shall praise Your works to another, And shall declare Your mighty acts. 5 I will meditate on the glorious splendor of Your majesty, And on Your wondrous works. 6 Men shall speak of the might of Your awesome acts, And I will declare Your greatness.

2 Peter 1:16—For we did not follow cunningly devised fables when we made known to you the power and coming of our Lord Jesus Christ, but were eyewitnesses of His majesty.

Jude 1:25—To God our Savior, Who alone is wise, Be glory and majesty, Dominion and power, Both now and forever. Amen.

OBJECTIONS & RESPONSES

None noted. See also the above arguments in this section.

PRACTICAL POINTS TO PONDER

1. Every pursuit for achieving greatness in life will fail or pale when compared to God's greatness.
2. God is unsurpassed in His greatness, and nothing or no one is greater.
3. There is no need for a continuous, and ultimately fruitless, search for anyone or anything other than the Majestic God.

NECESSITY

DEFINITION
God cannot not exist.

DESCRIPTION

God is Necessary Being. God cannot *not* exist because God is Pure Self-Existent Act. *Necessary* or *necessity* are also defined as logically inescapable, something that cannot be denied without contradiction, the quality or state of being in need (by someone or something), i.e., absolutely needed (*Merriam Webster*, with additions by the writer). Necessary Being necessarily implies that there is also contingent being.

While Necessary Being is independent of all else, *contingent* being is dependent on something or someone else for its being. In other words, it does not exist in and of itself, but needs someone or something apart from, and thus greater than, itself to exist.

As Necessary Being, God's non-existence is impossible, and His existence is essential. God simply does continually exist and cannot *not* exist. Contingent being(s), humans in particular, *can* not exist, for our existence is not essential, and our essence is not identical to our existence in this current, mortal form. Our essential nature is not decay, death, and separation from each other and God; instead, it is enduring, beautiful, and relational everlasting life with each other and God.

Necessity

ARGUMENTS

Contingent being can mean mortal being.
Mortal being means dependent being.
Dependent being needs something from an independent source.
An independent source is a self-existent source.
The only Self-Existent source is God.
Thus, contingent (mortal) being needs God.

I am unnecessary for the universe to exist.
But if I am unnecessary, that presumes something is necessary for the universe to exist.
God is Necessary for the universe to exist.

All humans are finite.
All finite are sustained by God.
All humans are sustained by God.

If human being, then contingent being.
Human being.
Thus, contingent being.

If contingent, then dependent.
Contingent.
Thus, dependent.

If dependent, then there is an Independent Source on which one depends.
Dependent.
Thus, there is an Independent Source on which one depends.

Either necessary or unnecessary.
Not necessary.
Therefore, unnecessary.

Either infinite being or dependent being.
Finite being.
Therefore, dependent being.

Either God depends on us for existence, or we depend on God for existence and everything else.
God does not depend on us for anything, including His existence.
Thus, we depend on God for existence and everything else.

SCRIPTURES

Genesis 1:27—So God created man in His own image; in the image of God He created him; male and female He created them.

Genesis 2:7—And the LORD God formed man of the dust of the ground, and breathed into his nostrils the breath of life; and man became a living being.

Psalm 50:10-12—10 For every beast of the forest is Mine, And the cattle on a thousand hills. 11 I know all the birds of the mountains, And the wild beasts of the field are Mine. 12 "If I were hungry, I would not tell you; For the world is Mine, and all its fullness."

1 Corinthians 11:11-12—11 Nevertheless, neither is man independent of woman, nor woman independent of man, in the Lord. 12 For as woman came from man, even so man also comes through woman; but all things are from God.

1 Corinthians 8:5-6—5 For even if there are so-called gods, whether in heaven or on earth (as there are many "gods" and many "lords"), 6 yet for us there is one God, the Father, of whom are all things, and we for Him; and one Lord Jesus Christ, through whom are all things, and through whom we live.

OBJECTIONS & RESPONSES

None noted. See also the above arguments in this section, "Theology Proper" and "Aseity."

PRACTICAL POINTS TO PONDER

1. God never needs us in order to be God, but we always need God in order to be us.
2. Because God is Necessary, He will always necessarily have what we need.
3. Though God is Necessary and will always have what we *need*, that does not necessarily mean that He will always give us what we *want*.
4. Because we need God, and God is unchangingly loving and faithful, we can also trust God to do exactly what He said He would do, according to His Word, the Bible.

OMNIPOTENT

DEFINITION
God is all-powerful.

DESCRIPTION

Omnipotence means "all power(ful)." This entails God as "Almighty," and "I am that I am," both of which ultimately refer to His Unlimited Self-Existence, meaning God is unlimited in all that He is, including His power. But because God is Omnipotent, it does not mean that God can do anything at all. There are things that God can and cannot do, according to His nature.

For example, God *cannot*:
- Perform actual contradictions against immutable, essential reality, e.g., make a square triangle, or deny Himself through lying about anything.
- Change His nature or essence, e.g., become less powerful, infinite, truthful, cease to exist, etc.
- Force someone to "love" Him, since love is a voluntary action of a free-willed agent.

God *can*:
- *Do* what is *actually* possible to do (e.g., create the universe *ex nihilo* from out of no pre-existing matter; heal the sick; raise the dead; etc.).
- *Limit* the use of His power, i.e., not unleash total oblivion upon the creation in distributing punishment.

- Do what He has not done, e.g., in His Wisdom, God may do somethings at some point of time that He has not previously done in time.

ARGUMENTS

What God is, God has.
God is Infinite and clearly has the power to create the cosmos.
Thus, God is Infinite Power, i.e., Omnipotent.

God has power.
God is Immense Being.
Immense is immeasurable.
Thus, God's power cannot be measured, i.e., God is Omnipotent.

God is Pure Act and is Self-Existent, Independent, Necessary Existence.
God simply exists in and of Himself.
Thus, God is Omnipotent.

If finite, then potential to not exist.
Finite.
Thus, potential to not exist.

If mortal, then limited.
Mortal.
Therefore, limited.

If humans did not come from an all-powerful Source, then they either come from some other limited power source or they are the source of all the power needed for their existence.

It is not the case that humans are the sole power source for their existence, for no human can cause or indefinitely sustain its own existence.
Neither has it been empirically or factually shown that there is some other limited power source of human beings that causes or indefinitely sustains their existence.
Thus, humans come from an all-powerful Source.

Either dependent and limited in power or independent and unlimited in power.
Not dependent and limited in power.
Thus, independent and unlimited in power.

Either potency or all-powerful.
Not all-powerful.
Thus, potency.

Either God is all-powerful, or God is not all-powerful, or there is no God.
It is not the case that God is not all-powerful (Infinite, Self-Existent).
It is not the case that God does not exist (all dependent beings need an Independent Cause).
Thus, God is all-powerful.

SCRIPTURES

Psalm 115:3—But our God is in heaven; He does whatever He pleases.

Psalm 147:5—Great is our Lord, and mighty in power; His understanding is infinite.

Jeremiah 32:17—Ah, Lord GOD! Behold, You have made the heavens and the earth by Your great power and outstretched arm. There is nothing too hard for You.

Luke 18:27—But He said, "The things which are impossible with men are possible with God."

John 10:17-18—17 "Therefore My Father loves Me, because I lay down My life that I may take it again. 18 No one takes it from Me, but I lay it down of Myself. I have power to lay it down, and I have power to take it again. This command I have received from My Father."

OBJECTIONS & RESPONSES

Objection 1: God has not eradicated evil, so God is impotent.

If God is all-powerful, then God would have eradicated all evil.
But evil still exists.
Therefore, God must not be all-powerful, i.e., God must be impotent and unable to eradicate all evil.

Response 1: God can and will one day eradicate all evil.

The study of the existence of God in light of the existence of evil is called *theodicy*. The argument noted above is a common one against God's Omnipotence. And while the argument is formally valid, it is not materially true.

Formal validity has to do with an argument's conclusion being supported by its premises. In the case of the previous hypothetical argument, it is formally valid because the conclusion is supported by its "if" premise called the *antecedent* (Geisler and Brooks, *Come*, 60-61). In addition, it properly denies the "then" part called the *consequent*; in formal logic, this is called *modus tollens* (Ibid). But, as previously noted, *formal* validity does not equal *material* correspondent truth.

Material truth corresponds to reality. The reality is that God can do what He has not done. God has not yet eradicated all evil because God is merciful towards those who commit evil, i.e., human beings. Because God has not eradicated evil yet does not mean that He will not eradicate it in the future. And this is exactly what the Bible reveals God will one day do (see 2 Peter 3:3-13).

PRACTICAL POINTS TO PONDER
1. God has the power to do whatever is *actually* possible to do.
2. God has the power to do what He *promised*.
3. God has the power to meet all of our *needs*.
4. God has the *power* to eradicate evil; the *will* to eradicate evil; and one day will eradicate *all* evil.

OMNISCIENT

DEFINITION

God is all-knowing.

DESCRIPTION

Omniscient means all-knowing. God's Omniscience flows from His Pure Self-Existence, which also includes His limitlessness in essence and being (Infinity). So, God is unlimited in knowledge as well. Omniscience is also defined as having infinite awareness, understanding, and insight, or to be in possession of universal or complete knowledge (*Merriam Webster*). It is to be all-knowing, all-wise, all-seeing, and all-perceiving (*Synonym Finder*).

God knows everything that is actually knowable and possible. God's knowledge is not *a posteriori*, i.e., after experience, or gained by material means. God knows all that can be done, but not by virtue of actually *doing* any or all of it Himself. God knows the who, what, when, where, why, and how we sin, but God does not *commit* sin. It is impossible for God to sin, for to sin would be to change from being holy to unholy, and God is Immutable. God knows that we have human frailties (hunger, aging, etc.), but not how those things feel, i.e., in His Divine Essence (however, as some may note, Jesus—God the Son—did know these things to some significant degree via His human incarnation).

ARGUMENTS

God is Self-Existent.
Self-Existent is Necessary Existence.
Necessary Existence is Infinite Existence.
Infinite Existence is Limitless Existence.
Limitless Existence is Limitless Knowledge.
God is Limitless Knowledge.

God is Necessary Being.
Necessary Being is the Efficient Cause of all contingent being.
As the Necessary Efficient Cause of all other being, God has all knowledge about all other being.
Thus, God is Omniscient.

If Infinite, then Omniscient.
Infinite.
Thus, Omniscient.

If God is not All-Knowing, then God is untrustworthy.
God is trustworthy.
Thus, God is All-Knowing.

If Jesus did not know the day He would return for the Rapture, then Jesus was not Omniscient and thus not God.
It is not the case that Jesus was not God.
Jesus was Omniscient in His Divine nature.
Thus, as God in His Divine nature, Jesus did—and does—know the day of the Rapture.

Either limited or unlimited.
Not limited.
Therefore, unlimited.

Omniscient

Either God knows everything that can be known, or God is not Omniscient.
God is Omniscient.
Thus, God knows everything that can be known.

Either God knows all things at all times, or God has to learn things at some time and is not Omniscient.
God does not learn at any time, for God is not limited by time or space, but is beyond time and space.
Thus, God knows all things at all times.

SCRIPTURES

John 2:24-25—24 But Jesus did not commit Himself to them, because He knew all men, 25 and had no need that anyone should testify of man, for He knew what was in man.

John 16:30—Now we are sure that You know all things, and have no need that anyone should question You. By this we believe that You came forth from God.

John 21:17—He said to him the third time, "Simon, son of Jonah, do you love Me?" Peter was grieved because He said to him the third time, "Do you love Me?" And he said to Him, "Lord, You know all things; You know that I love You." Jesus said to him, "Feed My sheep!"

Hebrews 4:13—And there is no creature hidden from His sight, but all things are naked and open to the eyes of Him to whom we must give account.

James 1:5—If any of you lacks wisdom, let him ask of God, who gives to all liberally and without reproach, and it will be given to him.

OBJECTIONS & RESPONSES

Objection 1: Praying to an Omniscient God is ridiculous.

Since God knows everything, then there is no need to pray to God. Even the Bible says in Matthew 6:8 that God knows what we need even before we ask. Therefore, praying to God is ridiculous and useless.

Response 1: Praying to the Omniscient God is not ridiculous.

This is a common misunderstanding about prayer among many Christians, and perhaps non-Christians as well. Prayer is not simply a *one-way* communication to God in either asking Him for things or telling Him what is going on with us. Prayer is a *dialogue* between two people—God and the one praying. Prayer establishes and builds relationship with God. Just because God knows what we need does not mean that we should not ask. The Bible also says in Matthew 7:7 to "ask, and it will be given to you; seek, and you will find; knock, and it will be opened to you."

Objection 2: Jesus did not know the time of the Rapture and thus is not God.

Jesus, who is said to be God, did not know the timing of the Rapture. He said only the "father" knew (Matthew 24:36). Thus, if Jesus did not know about the Rapture, then that makes Jesus non-omniscient and not God.

Response 2: Jesus Christ has two natures.

Remember that Jesus is two "what's" in one "who." He is God the Son, who took on a body of flesh, and dwelt among humans (e.g., John 1:14). Jesus Christ was born, then grew up, died, and was resurrected with respect to His human nature. His divine nature as God the Son, who existed before the world was (John 17:5) and through whom all the worlds were made (John 1:1-2; Hebrews 1:2), is not, and cannot be, limited in knowledge. Thus, Jesus Christ was limited in knowledge in His physical human nature, but not in His divine nature.

Objection 3: God's Omniscience destroys free will.

If God knows everything people will ever do, then we really do not have free will to do anything. We are just pawns in the hands of a playful deity.

Response 3: God's Omniscience does not control our actions.

Just because God knows everything in no way means that God *determines* or *forces* us to do them. Humans are free to do what we are actually able to do; to become what we are actually able to become; and to think the fantastic number of things that we are able to think. God does not *make* us do, become, or think. But God does *know* what we will do, become, or think. God's knowing does not determine our doing, being, or thinking. Our individual will does.

PRACTICAL POINTS TO PONDER

1. God knows how the universe works because God made it.
2. God knows what we are going through and knows what to do to help us.
3. God knows what we need and knows how to meet every one of our needs.

PURE ACT / EXISTENCE

DEFINITION

God is pure existence.

DESCRIPTION

God as *Pure Actuality* or *Existence* can be difficult for us to grasp. Relative to living, most of our existence revolves around a beginning, a duration of some sort, then an ending. When investigating physical things, we can clearly discern a starting point; an extension in both space and time; and an endpoint of the space that the object fills. But God's Pure Actuality / Existence is not actually *comprehensible*, i.e., fully understood by our senses, but is logically *apprehensible*, i.e., able to be grasped in some way by our minds.

Logically speaking, something cannot come from nothing. Something or someone else must be the cause. Anything that is caused is contingent. Since the thing caused is contingent, then at some point its cause must be non-contingent. And that cause must not have, or need, a cause itself. That would make it uncaused. Any non-contingent, uncaused being must, of necessity, exist in and of itself, and not be bound by space or time.

Therefore, God is the Uncaused, Self-Existent Primary Efficient First Cause of all else, and as such simply is—and from a human perspective, always has been and will be—God. If there were no Purely Self-Existent God, we would not exist. This does not mean that we would be merely devoid of biological life. This does mean that neither we, nor other contingent being(s), would have any particles or atoms in the universe. We simply would not be at all.

ARGUMENTS

If Infinite, then Pure Existence.
Infinite.
Therefore, Pure Existence.

If God exists because humans say so, then God's existence is dependent on human beings.
God's existence is not dependent on human beings.
Therefore, God does not exist simply because humans say so (i.e., God exists because God is Pure Existence).

If God is Pure Existence, then only God knows how old He is.
But God cannot know how old He is because God does not exist in time, and aging only occurs in time. God is also Spirit, so God has no physical parts in space in order to age in time. This is an informal logical fallacy of a *category mistake*, i.e., putting the Eternal, Infinite, Spirit God into the category of temporal, finite, physical things.
Therefore, God is Pure Unaging and Ageless Existence.

Either created or Creator.
Not created.
Thus, Creator.

Either caused or Uncaused.
Not caused.
Therefore, Uncaused.

Either God simply exists in and of Himself, or God is caused by someone or something greater than Himself.

Pure Act / Existence

But God is Infinite in essence, so there can be no greater existence than He.

Thus, God simply exists in and of Himself.

SCRIPTURES

Genesis 1:1—In the beginning God created the heavens and the earth.

Exodus 3:14—God said to Moses, "I am who I am . This is what you are to say to the Israelites: 'I AM has sent me to you.' "

John 8:58—"I tell you the truth," Jesus answered, "before Abraham was born, I am!"

John 10:30-33—30 I and My Father are one." 31 Then the Jews took up stones again to stone Him. 32 Jesus answered them, "Many good works I have shown you from My Father. For which of those works do you stone Me?" 33 The Jews answered Him, saying, "For a good work we do not stone You, but for blasphemy, and because You, being a Man, make Yourself God."

John 17:5—And now, Father, glorify me in your presence with the glory I had with you before the world began.

Colossians 1:16-17—16 For by him all things were created: things in heaven and on earth, visible and invisible, whether thrones or powers or rulers or authorities; all things were created by him and for him. 17 He is before all things, and in him all things hold together.

OBJECTIONS & RESPONSES

None noted. See also the above arguments in this section, "Theology Proper" and "Aseity."

PRACTICAL POINTS TO PONDER

1. God's existence is independent of everything else, so He can never be unduly influenced or coerced by anyone.
2. God is real and He is active in the universe.
3. God is real and He is active in our lives each day.
4. Because He cannot not exist, God will always be with us to help, guide, direct, instruct, correct, console, encourage, rescue, redeem, and one day rapture us.

SIMPLE

DEFINITION

God is one essential being with no parts.

DESCRIPTION

There is only One True God. When speaking of God as "simple," one speaks regarding God's uncomplicated being (essence). In other words, there is no complexity to the essence of God. God "simply is." It also connotes that there are not two or more "component parts" in God (as implied by pantheism and panentheism).

The word "simple" is an alteration of Latin *simplic-, simplex*, meaning single, having one ingredient, plain. It is also from sem-, *sim*, meaning one + -plic-, -plex, which means "fold." It also means "not limited or restricted" (*Merriam Webster*).

Synonymously, it means single, uncombined, uncompounded, uncomplex, simplex, unalloyed, unmixed, unblended, sole, only, pure" (*The Synonym Finder*).

It is important to note here what simplicity does and does not mean regarding the nature and existence of God.

Simplicity does *not* mean that:
- God cannot *be* three Persons in one Essential Being.
- God cannot *have* many attributes and characteristics.
- God cannot *do* many things.

Simplicity *does* mean that:
- God *is* three Persons in one Essential Being.
- God *does* have many discernible attributes within His Essence.
- God can only *be* One thing, i.e., Simple, but God can *do* many things.

ARGUMENTS

God is the only Uncaused, Self-Existent, Primary Efficient First Cause. As such God is Pure Existence.
What is Pure is simple.
Thus, God is Simple Existence.

God is Simple Existence.
What is Simple has no parts.
Thus, God has no parts.

All of God's Essence is pure.
Simple necessarily entails only what is pure.
Thus, God's essence is simple.

If parts, then not simple.
Parts.
Thus, not simple.

If God can be "parted," then God is divisible and not simple.
God is Infinite Essence and Immortal, thus indivisible—for how could one traverse actual infinitude in order to divide it?
Therefore, it must necessarily be the case that God has no parts, i.e., is Simple.

If something has "parts," it exists in space and time.
But God is beyond space and time.
Therefore, God has no parts in Himself, i.e., is Simple.

Either simple or complex.
Not complex.
Thus, simple.

Either God is Simple Being, or God is non-Simple Being.
It is not the case that God is non-Simple, i.e., "complex," Being. God is Pure Being, which logically denotes non-complexity.
Thus, God is Simple Being.

Either God has parts and is a physical being, or God has no parts and is Simple Being.
It is not the case that God is a physical being, for physical beings exist in time and are extended in space (i.e., occupy it).
God is beyond space and time.
Thus, God has no parts and is Simple Being.

SCRIPTURES

Deuteronomy 6:4—Hear, O Israel: The LORD our God, the LORD is one!

Isaiah 43:10—"You are My witnesses," says the LORD, "and My servant whom I have chosen, that you may know and believe Me, and understand that I am He. Before Me there was no God formed, nor shall there be after Me."

Isaiah 44:6—Thus says the LORD, the King of Israel, and his Redeemer, the LORD of hosts: 'I am the First and I am the Last; besides Me there is no God.'

Isaiah 45:8—For thus says the LORD, who created the heavens, who is God, who formed the earth and made it, who has established it, who did not create it in vain, who formed it to be inhabited: "I am the LORD, and there is no other."

1 Timothy 2:5—For there is one God and one Mediator between God and men, the Man Christ Jesus.

OBJECTIONS & RESPONSES

Objection 1: The Bible says God has body parts.

There are many places in the Bible that say God has "eyes, hands, feet, ears, a heart, a mind," etc. These clearly are all "parts." So, either God really has parts or the Bible is inaccurate—and maybe even untrue—when it describes what God is.

Response 1: Figures of Speech do not mean that God has actual human characteristics.

It is true that the Bible has many verses that speak of God in human terms. For example, Genesis 6:8 for "eyes"; Genesis 3:8 for "walking"; 1 Samuel 5:11 for "hand," etc..

However, these are figures of speech called *anthropomorphisms* (Zuck, *Basic*, 151), meaning that human attributes are ascribed to non-human entities, like God in those previously noted cases (*metaphor* is also used, e.g., as noted in "Light").

Just as no one reasonably thinks that a person was actually on fire when a sports report says that a certain player "was on fire" during the athletic activity—but instead clearly means the person was playing at a very high level—neither should anyone take out of context figures of speech in the Bible about anything or anyone in general, and about God in particular. Just as "mountains," "heavens," and "forests" do not literally "sing"—at least not in the same way that human beings sing—neither should one believe that God, in Essence, has human or other physical attributes.

Objection 2: Jesus, who is God had body parts, thus, God is not simple.

One of the main parts—if not *the* main part—of Christian belief and doctrine is the deity of Jesus Christ. This means that Jesus Christ was actually "God," who came down to earth in a physical body, and "in Him [dwelled] all the fullness of the Godhead bodily," as in Colossians 2:9. Now, if Jesus was actually a real person, then Jesus clearly had parts. But if Jesus Christ was God, then that means God had parts. So, if God had parts, then God cannot be "one simple essence."

Response 2: Jesus Christ has two natures.

Remember that Jesus is two "what's" in one "who." He is God the Son, who took on a body of flesh, and dwelt among humans (e.g., John 1:14). Jesus Christ was born, then grew up, died, and was resurrected with respect to His human nature. Clearly, in the incarnation, Jesus had body parts. But in His eternally divine nature as God the Son, who existed before the world was (John 17:5) and through whom all the worlds were made (John 1:1-2; Hebrews 1:2), Jesus could not possibly have had any physical parts.

That the "fullness of the Godhead" dwelled in Him "bodily" speaks to the uniqueness of Jesus among any other existing person, rather than an expression of an essential limitation via the incarnation. Neither does it reveal a deficiency in the essence of God as Simple, Pure Being. Again, Jesus was the first, last, and only being who was fully human and fully God. This does not go *against* human reason, but *beyond* it. Thus, the incarnation of God in Christ Jesus does not mean that God is not Pure Simple Being.

PRACTICAL POINTS TO PONDER
1. God is absolutely, indivisibly One God.
2. God is the only God; all else are false gods.
3. We should not focus on anything less than God, i.e., idols, for our sustenance and fulfillment.

TRINITY

DEFINITION

God is Three Persons in one Essential being.

DESCRIPTION

God as "triune" or a holy *Trinity* is a uniquely biblical concept that is hermeneutically clear and evident in the Holy Bible. It seems highly unlikely that anyone would conceive of God as Three Persons in one Essential Being apart from the revelation of the Holy Writ.

The cognitive dissonance in the minds of many about God as Trinity is often associated with the inability of the human mind to overcome the presupposition of univocal human personhood, i.e., one person in one human essence. As human beings participate in God's Being and, biblically, are similar in personhood to Him, we should reconsider the definition of our personhood relative to the Person from whom we received it. Personhood, as it exists in God, must necessarily be devoid of mere physicality, as God is not physical, i.e., He is essentially not located in space-time.

Personhood for human beings, as our personhood is derived from God, should primarily revolve around the non-corporeal qualities given to us from God, i.e., thoughts, feelings, free will, etc. Our personhood is *more* than our sole physical existence. God's Personhood is essentially beyond mere physical instantiation. The Immaterial God (no parts, no physicality) is Triune Personhood within essential noncorporeal Essence.

It is important at this point to delineate between what "Trinity" means and does not mean.

Trinity does *not* mean:
- That there are three gods in Christianity; that is Tritheism.
- That God exists in three "modes" at different times, i.e., never is Father, Son, and Holy Spirit all the time at the same time; that is *modalism* or *Sabellianism*.
- That there are three persons in one person, which is a contradiction.

Trinity *does* mean:
- God is three Persons in one Essence.
- God is a plurality within a unity.
- God is three "Whos" in one "What."

ARGUMENTS

Either Pure Being or non-Pure Being
Not non-Pure Being.
Therefore, Pure Being.

If Pure Being, then One Essential Being.
Pure Being.
Therefore, One Essential Being.

The Holy Spirit existed before the world was created.
Jesus Christ, God the Son, existed before the world was created.
God the Father existed before the world was created.
Only One God existed before the world was created.
The Father, Son, and Holy Spirit are the One Essential God who existed before the world was created.

SCRIPTURES

Genesis 1:1-2—1 In the beginning God created the heavens and the earth. 2 The earth was without form, and void; and darkness was on the face of the deep. And the Spirit of God was hovering over the face of the waters.

John 1:1-3—1 In the beginning was the Word, and the Word was with God, and the Word was God. 2 He was in the beginning with God. 3 All things were made through Him, and without Him nothing was made that was made.

Matthew 3:16-17—16 When He had been baptized, Jesus came up immediately from the water; and behold, the heavens were opened to Him, and He saw the Spirit of God descending like a dove and alighting upon Him. 17 And suddenly a voice came from heaven, saying, "This is My beloved Son, in whom I am well pleased."

1 Corinthians 2:10-11—10 But God has revealed them to us through His Spirit. For the Spirit searches all things, yes, the deep things of God. 11 For what man knows the things of a man except the spirit of the man which is in him? Even so no one knows the things of God except the Spirit of God.

John 10:30-33—30 I and My Father are one." 31 Then the Jews took up stones again to stone Him. 32 Jesus answered them, "Many good works I have shown you from My Father. For which of those works do you stone Me?" 33 The Jews answered Him, saying, "For a good work we do not stone You, but for blasphemy, and because You, being a Man, make Yourself God."

OBJECTIONS & RESPONSES

Objection 1: It is not possible for three to equal one.

It is logically impossible for three to equal one. Therefore, it is logically impossible for "three persons" to equal "one person," as the so-called Christian Trinity is said for "Three Persons to equal One God."

Response 1: It is logically and mathematically possible for three to equal one.

If the biblically revealed Christian doctrine of the Trinity stated that there are "Three Gods in One God," i.e., that three of one thing is the same as exactly one thing, then that would be a logical impossibility. However, the biblically revealed doctrine of the Trinity essentially states that God is One Divine Being, eternally existent in Three Persons, and vice versa, which is not a logical impossibility. Even so, mathematically, one times one times one times one—even *ad infinitum*—will always only equal one. Likewise, one divided by one—*ad infinitum*—would always only equal one. Thus, there is no mathematical impossibility of many instances of "one" being equal to "one."

Though either of the three aforementioned examples may be actually *incomprehensible* to the human mind, they are nevertheless possible, and thus *apprehensible* by the human mind. In short, they serve as reasonable, apprehensible, analogical examples of God's Triunity.

PRACTICAL POINTS TO PONDER

1. God's Triunity is possible because personhood goes beyond mere physicality.
2. God is absolutely, indivisibly One God.
3. It accords with Scripture regarding how Jesus' death in His humanity (via the incarnation) does not mean that God died in His Divinity (Jesus as God the Son).
4. God is the only God; all else are false gods.

UNITY

DEFINITION
God is one essential being.

DESCRIPTION
Unity is defined as the quality or state of not being multiple. It is continuity without deviation or change (*Merriam Webster*). Synonymously, it means singleness, singularity, wholeness, homogeneity, sameness, harmony, agreement, fellowship, oneness (*The Synonym Finder*).

God is One Essential Being. This means that God's essence is indivisible. In relation to God, unity means "Oneness." God alone is the One True God, and thus only God should be worshipped. Of necessity, this excludes *polytheism*, which says there are many "gods" to worship. It also excludes *tri-theism*, which says there are three "gods" to worship, and excludes *idolatry*, which says that any (false) "god" can be worshipped. This concept is inextricably related with God as Simple and Tri-une (Trinity). Thomas Aquinas says in Summa Theologica, 1a.11.4:

> "Since 'one' is an undivided being, if anything is supremely 'one' it must be supremely being, and supremely undivided. Now both of these belong to God. For He is supremely being, inasmuch as His being is not determined by any nature to which it is adjoined; since He is being itself, subsistent, absolutely undetermined. But He is supremely undivided inasmuch as He is divided neither actually nor potentially, by

any mode of division; since He is altogether simple . . . Hence it is manifest that God is 'one' in the supreme degree."

ARGUMENTS

God is Unchanging Being.
Unchanging Being is unchangeable unity.
God is unchangeable Unity.

Either unified or multiplied.
Not multiplied.
Therefore, unified.

If God's Being is multiple, then God is not one single Unity in Being.
Logically, philosophically, and biblically, God is only One God, i.e., Unity of Being.
Therefore, God is not multiple Being.

SCRIPTURES

Deuteronomy 6:4—"Hear, O Israel: The Lord our God, the Lord is one!

Isaiah 44:6—"Thus says the Lord, the King of Israel, And his Redeemer, the Lord of hosts: 'I am the First and I am the Last; Besides Me there is no God.

Revelation 1:8—"I am the Alpha and the Omega, the Beginning and the End," says the Lord, "who is and who was and who is to come, the Almighty."

Revelation 22:12-13—12 "And behold, I am coming quickly, and My reward is with Me, to give to every one according to his work. 13 I am the Alpha and the Omega, the Beginning and the End, the First and the Last."

John 10:30-33—30 I and My Father are one." 31 Then the Jews took up stones again to stone Him. 32 Jesus answered them, "Many good works I have shown you from My Father. For which of those works do you stone Me?" 33 The Jews answered Him, saying, "For a good work we do not stone You, but for blasphemy, and because You, being a Man, make Yourself God."

OBJECTIONS & RESPONSES

See "Simple," "Triune" and the above arguments in this section.

PRACTICAL POINTS TO PONDER

1. God is absolutely, indivisibly One God.
2. We should not focus on anything less than God, e.g., idols, for our sustenance and fulfillment.
3. As there is eternally perfect unity and fellowship in the Godhead, there should be greater unity and fellowship between members in the Body of Christ, and the Body of Christ with God.

WISDOM

DEFINITION

God knows the best means to the best end.

DESCRIPTION

Theologically, *wisdom* is accurately defined by God's unerringly knowing and providing the best means to the best end. It is also defined as the ability to discern inner qualities and relationships: insight marked by deep understanding, keen discernment, and a capacity for sound judgment (*Merriam Webster*). Synonymously, it means discerning, perspicacious, sapient, insightful, reasonable, brilliant (*The Synonym Finder*).

Wisdom aligns with God as Infinite, Omnipotent, and Omniscient. God has no limit to His Being, and therefore neither to His knowledge or power. As such, God knows every way that can be known to accomplish the best end for everything and everyone in the cosmos, and has the power to make it come to pass.

ARGUMENTS

Either all-wise or unknowing.
Not unknowing.
Therefore, all-wise.

God is Infinite.
God is Wise.
God is Infinite Wisdom.

God is Omniscient.
God is Omnipotent.
God knows all that can be known and can do all that can be done.
Thus, God knows the best means to the best end, i.e., is Wisdom.

God knows all that can be known.
God can do all that can (righteously) be done.
Thus, God knows and guides without error, i.e., is Wise.

SCRIPTURES

Job 12:13—With Him are wisdom and strength, He has counsel and understanding.

Jeremiah 10:12—He has made the earth by His power, He has established the world by His wisdom, and has stretched out the heavens at His discretion.

James 1:5—If any of you lacks wisdom, let him ask of God, who gives to all liberally and without reproach, and it will be given to him.

James 3:13-17—13 Who is wise and understanding among you? Let him show by good conduct that his works are done in the meekness of wisdom. 14 But if you have bitter envy and self-seeking in your hearts, do not boast and lie against the truth. 15 This wisdom does not descend from above, but is earthly, sensual, demonic. 16 For where envy and self-seeking exist, confusion and every evil thing are there. 17 But the wisdom that is from above is first pure, then peaceable, gentle, willing to yield, full of mercy and good fruits, without partiality and without hypocrisy.

Proverbs 2:6-7—6 For the Lord gives wisdom; From His mouth come knowledge and understanding; 7 He stores up sound wisdom for the upright; He is a shield to those who walk uprightly.

OBJECTIONS & RESPONSES

See "Objections" under "Omniscient," "Omnipotent," and "Infinite."

PRACTICAL POINTS TO PONDER

1. God knows all that can be known at all times.
2. God has all power to do what needs to be done at any time.
3. God can, and will, always do what is best for us at the right time, every time.

OMNIPRESENT

DEFINITION
God is in all places at all times.

DESCRIPTION
God's *Omnipresence* means that God is, in His Essence, in all places at all times. This is a non-moral characteristic of God, i.e., what God is relative to the physical, created universe. God's Omnipresence denotes that God is nowhere absent. There is no place in existence where God is not able to be, and where God is not. God is everywhere present.

This characteristic of God comes from Self-Existence, Infinity, Eternality, and Immateriality. God exists in and of Himself, created everything in space and time, is not limited by space nor time, is Spirit, and thus, is able to be everywhere present.

ARGUMENTS
If Immaterial, then Spirit.
If Spirit, then non-spatial.
If non-spatial, then timeless.
If timeless, then eternal.
If eternal, then unlimited.
If unlimited, then self-existent.
If self-existent, then beyond time and space.
If beyond time and space, then not limited by time nor space.
God is Spirt that is not limited by time nor space.
Thus, God is Omnipresent.

Either Omnipresent or spatially limited.
Not spatially limited.
Therefore, Omnipresent.

God is Omniscient.
To be Omniscient is to have extant knowledge of all things in all places at all times.
Therefore, God is also Omnipresent.

SCRIPTURES

Psalm 33:13-15—13 The LORD looks from heaven; He sees all the sons of men. 14 From the place of His dwelling He looks on all the inhabitants of the earth; 15 He fashions their hearts individually; He considers all their works.

Psalm 139:7-8—7 Where can I go from Your Spirit? Or where can I flee from Your presence? 8 If I ascend into heaven, You are there; If I make my bed in hell, behold, You are there.

Proverbs 5:21—For the ways of man are before the eyes of the LORD, And He ponders all his paths.

Proverbs 15:3—The eyes of the LORD are in every place, keeping watch on the evil and the good.

Hebrews 4:13—And there is no creature hidden from His sight, but all things are naked and open to the eyes of Him to whom we must give account.

OBJECTIONS & RESPONSES

None noted. See also the above arguments in this section, "Theology Proper," "Immaterial," "Infinite," and "Simple."

PRACTICAL POINTS TO PONDER

1. There is no *place* where God's presence is not.
2. There is no *time* where God's being is not present.
3. You can have great comfort in the fact that at all times and in all places, God is wherever you are.

IMMANENT

DEFINITION

God is everywhere near.

DESCRIPTION

God's *Immanence* means that God is, in His Essence, everywhere near as the Sustaining Cause of any and all entities—both visible and invisible—at all times. Immanence, like Omnipresence, is a non-moral characteristic of God, i.e., what God is relative to the physical, created universe. God's Immanence denotes that God, in His Pure Actuality, i.e., Pure Isness, is simply always sustaining every created entity, and anything that is associated with every created entity. It means that nothing exists apart from God's Sustaining Power and Presence.

This characteristic of God comes from Self-Existence, Infinity, Eternality, Omniscience, Wisdom, and Omnipotence. God exists in and of Himself, is unlimited in knowledge, presence, and power, and having created everything in space and time, God is not limited by either. Since God is the Uncaused First Cause, and is eternally existent, every dependent thing must necessarily depend on Him, and God, of His very nature, is ever-present and near to fulfill their existential dependence.

ARGUMENTS

God is One Indivisible Being.
God is Omnipresent Being.
God's Being is equally everywhere at all times.
God is Immanent Being.

If God is indivisible, unlimited Being, then God also is Immanent Being.
God is both of those things.
Therefore, God is Immanent Being.

Either everywhere near at all times or in some places more than others at different times than others.
But if God is in more places than others at different times than others, then there is a deficiency in God at some time and some place than at other times and in other places, i.e., there is "less" of God.
And if there is "less of God" at any time and in any place, then God is somehow "limited" at that time and in that place.
However, God is Unlimited, Eternal, Omnipotent, and Omnipresent.
God is not limited by space nor time in any place at any time.
Therefore, God is everywhere near at all times, i.e., Immanent.

SCRIPTURES

Deuteronomy 4:7—"For what great nation is there that has God so near to it, as the Lord our God is to us, for whatever reason we may call upon Him?

1 Samuel 14:36—Now Saul said, "Let us go down after the Philistines by night, and plunder them until the morning light; and let us not leave a man of them." And they said, "Do whatever seems good to you." Then the priest said, "Let us draw near to God here."

Psalm 73:28—But it is good for me to draw near to God; I have put my trust in the Lord God, That I may declare all Your works.

Jeremiah 23:23-24—23 "Am I a God near at hand," says the Lord, "And not a God afar off? 24 Can anyone hide himself in secret places, So I shall not see him?" says the Lord; "Do I not fill heaven and earth?" says the Lord.

Acts 17:26-27—26 And He has made from one blood every nation of men to dwell on all the face of the earth, and has determined their preappointed times and the boundaries of their dwellings, 27 so that they should seek the Lord, in the hope that they might grope for Him and find Him, though He is not far from each one of us.

OBJECTIONS & RESPONSES

See "Omnipresent" and the above arguments in this section.

PRACTICAL POINTS TO PONDER

1. God's presence is not limited by space nor time; God is greater than space-time because God created space-time.
2. God is everywhere near at all times.
3. There is *nowhere* you are at any time where God is not *all-there* with you, to be God *for* you.

TRANSCENDENT

DEFINITION

God is greater than all of creation.

DESCRIPTION

Transcendent means to be beyond all limits and actual comprehension, i.e., that the physical, material universe is unable to contain the essence or existence of something. This could apply to none other than God. As Pure and Majestic Being, God is completely above, over, and beyond the created cosmos. And since this is true, any statement to the contrary belies the very nature of God, proving to be false. For example, if God is not Omnipotent, then God could possibly be subject to the creation He has made; this is the view of *Finite Godism*. In addition, if God is actually the physical universe itself—everything is God, and God is everything—then God is, again, limited in His Being, and thus not Transcendent; the former is the view of *Pantheism* (all is God), also called *monism* (God = all, therefore, all = God = all is one).

In addition to Pure Being, God's Aseity, Infinity, Immortality, Immateriality, Omnipotence, and Omniscience all lead to His Transcendence. God's Unlimited Self-Existence means that He is ever-living and unbound by space or time. As such, His knowledge and power are without end, and He is undoubtedly over every entity in the universe.

ARGUMENTS

God is Infinite, Self-Existent, All-Powerful, Eternal, Immortal, Immaterial, Omniscient Being.
Thus, God is Transcendent.

If mortal, then contingent.
If contingent, then dependent.
If dependent, then limited.
If limited, then non-transcendent.
God is Immortal, Self-Existent, Infinite Being.
Therefore, God is Transcendent.

Either ruling over everything or ruled by something.
Not ruled by anything.
Therefore, ruling over everything.

SCRIPTURES

1 Chronicles 29:11—Yours, O LORD, is the greatness, The power and the glory, The victory and the majesty; for all that is in heaven and in earth is Yours; Yours is the kingdom, O LORD, And You are exalted as head over all.

Psalm 8:1—O LORD, our Lord, How excellent is Your name in all the earth, Who have set Your glory above the heavens!

Psalm 57:5—Be exalted, O God, above the heavens; let Your glory be above all the earth.

Psalm 97:9—For You, LORD, are most high above all the earth; You are exalted far above all gods.

Psalm 113:4—The Lord is high above all nations, His glory above the heavens.

OBJECTIONS & RESPONSES

None noted. See also the above arguments in this section, as well as "Majesty," "Pure Being / Act," "Omnipotence," "Omniscience," and "Aseity."

PRACTICAL POINTS TO PONDER

1. God created the universe and is not limited by, nor an essential part of, the universe.
2. God is imminently greater than all the powers, and even limitations, of the universe.
3. God is able to do exceedingly and abundantly above all that you can ask or even imagine.

SOVEREIGN

DEFINITION

God controls all of creation.

DESCRIPTION

To be *sovereign* is to have complete control and authority. When speaking of God as Sovereign, the former things are entailed, but God's Sovereignty should be primarily understood as God having unsurpassed *power*. Nothing or no one anywhere or at any time was, is, or will be more powerful than God. God rules over creation in a way that is totally impossible for any other being. God is ultimately in control of everything. God is the Efficient Cause, i.e., "the" Causer of events, wherein He either *allows* or *directs* particular things to happen—both moral (right or wrong) or non-moral (the physical universe)—while at the same time sustaining everything in the universe, i.e., actively causing it to exist at any given time, all the time.

God's Sovereignty is closely aligned with, and inseparably bound to, His Transcendence. Because God is Uncaused, Self-Existent, and Unlimited in Being, God is Omnipotent, Omniscient, All-Wise, and Eternal. Thus, God can, and does, have everlasting authority *over* and *in* the entire cosmos, and is unsurpassed in power, relative to the creation. God is Sovereign.

ARGUMENTS

Either all-powerful or possibly subject to a greater power.
Not subject to a greater power.

Thus, all-powerful.

If human will can override God's will, then humans are more powerful than God.
But humans are finite, mortal, dependent, and limited beings, none of which applies to God.
Humans are not more powerful than God.
Therefore, human will cannot, and does not ever, override God's will.
God is Sovereign.

God is All-Wise.
Humans are often unwise.
Therefore, the All-Wise God does not acquiesce to often unwise humans.

SCRIPTURES

Exodus 15:18—"The Lord shall reign forever and ever."

1 Chronicles 29:12—Both riches and honor come from You, And You reign over all. In Your hand is power and might; In Your hand it is to make great and to give strength to all.

Psalm 47:8—God reigns over the nations; God sits on His holy throne.

Psalm 93:1—The Lord reigns, He is clothed with majesty; The Lord is clothed, He has girded Himself with strength. Surely the world is established, so that it cannot be moved.

Luke 1:31-33—31 And behold, you will conceive in your womb and bring forth a Son, and shall call His name Jesus. 32 He will be great, and will be called the Son of the Highest; and the Lord God will give

Him the throne of His father David. 33 And He will reign over the house of Jacob forever, and of His kingdom there will be no end."

OBJECTIONS & RESPONSES

See "Transcendent," "Anthropology" and the above arguments in this section.

PRACTICAL POINTS TO PONDER

1. God cannot be controlled by anything or anyone.
2. God is only always unfailingly God, and will unerringly, eternally act in accord with what He is.
3. God will always act in Love, Mercy, and Justice towards you at all times and in all circumstances; none can meaningfully oppose Him.

LOVE

DEFINITION

God is unfailingly devoted to the good of humankind.

DESCRIPTION

In one sense, "to love" is to express affection, devotion, and appreciation for someone or something. In another sense, it can be said that "to be love" is to have an unfailing, inescapable, unchanging, unending ability to both express affectionate devotion and to be the actual source of the same. It is to be unflinchingly committed to the "good" of someone or something. This is the measure in which God can be aptly defined as "love." God is *Love*.

In His essential Immutable goodness, God can only ever do what is in the best interests of the cosmos, including humankind. The inanimate cosmos, in its aesthetic beauty and complexity, reflects Gods love. Humankind, in its beautiful complexity, both reflects, receives and can imitate God's love.

Human actions do not change God's love towards us. God is Infinite and Eternal. Thus, God's love for humankind is not bound by place, space, time, nor circumstance. When God loves, it is not based on what *people* are, but what God *is*: always unfailingly, unchangingly devoted to doing what is best for us. God is love. And God does love.

ARGUMENTS

All sinners are loved by God.
All who are saved were at some time sinners.
All who are saved are loved by God.

God is love.
Love is unfailing.
God is unfailing love.

God is good.
Good is love.
God is love.

If good is love and God is good, then God is love.
God is good.
Thus, God is love.

If there is no God, then there is no love.
It is not the case that there is no love.
Therefore, it is not the case that there is no God.

If love among humans increases, then good among humans increases.
Good is not increasing.
Thus, love among humans is not increasing.

SCRIPTURES

Proverbs 3:12—For whom the Lord loves He corrects, Just as a father the son in whom he delights.

Jeremiah 31:3—The Lord has appeared of old to me, saying: "Yes, I have loved you with an everlasting love; therefore with lovingkindness I have drawn you."

John 3:16—For God so loved the world that He gave His only begotten Son, that whoever believes in Him should not perish but have everlasting life.

Romans 5:8—But God demonstrates His own love toward us, in that while we were still sinners, Christ died for us.

1 John 4:16—And we have known and believed the love that God has for us. God is love, and he who abides in love abides in God, and God in him.

OBJECTIONS & RESPONSES

None noted. See also the above arguments in this section.

PRACTICAL POINTS TO PONDER

1. God is Immanent and Omnipresent, so you are always near and surrounded by God's love.
2. God is Infinite and Eternal. There is never any limit to God's love for you.
3. God is Merciful and All-Good. God will forgive your sins and seek to restore, repair, and renew relationship with you.
4. God is always love, so you are always loved by God.

HOLY

DEFINITION

God cannot accept, nor be tainted by, sin.

DESCRIPTION

To be "holy" is to be set apart. God is *Holy*. This is not merely a matter of how God acts or behaves in a moral sense—as such things apply to free moral agents, i.e., human and spirit beings—but about what God *is* within Himself. God is Holy because God—in His Aseity, Infinity, Eternality, Immateriality, Necessity, and Pure Actuality—is Immutably Righteous (Just) and All-good. Any actions that breach God's prescribed righteousness is sin. God can mercifully *tolerate*, but never fully *accept*, sin. In addition, because God is Immutable and Immaterial, God is not tainted by sin.

God, in Essence, is totally set apart from creation. He is the Efficient Cause *of* it, but is in no way existentially bound or affected *by* it. Neither the physical machinations of the cosmos, nor the malevolent misdeeds of its free moral agents, affect God's essential Being. God remains Righteous despite the undeniable fact that free moral agents have been, are now, and will be, *unrighteous*, apart from faith in Jesus Christ.

No free moral agent can be set apart, i.e., made holy, by a mere act of that individual's will. Holiness, also called *sanctification*, is granted by God to those whom He sets apart according to His will for temporal purposes (e.g., Nebachudnezzar) or is applied to those who have faith in Jesus Christ (who is available to, but not accepted by, all people). When human beings are set apart by God, there is an expectation to obey, serve, and live for God, i.e., an expectation to be holy.

ARGUMENTS

God is Immaterial and Eternal.
What is Immaterial and Eternal is not spatio-temporal.
What is not spatio-temporal can be materially or actually affected by nothing outside itself, for it is essentially, totally separate from all else.
God is essentially, totally separate from all else.
Thus, God is Holy.

There is actualized goodness done by people in this world.
But people in this world are finite and contingent.
Therefore, goodness cannot originate with people.
Goodness must have a source that is greater than people.
God is greater than people.
Therefore, God is the Source of goodness.

If the God is the Source of goodness, then God is also the Source of Righteousness.
God is the Source of goodness.
Thus, God is also the Source of Righteousness.

Either set apart by God and holy, or set apart by God and unholy, or not set apart by God and holy.
One cannot be set apart by God but remain unholy forever, for that is a contradiction of what holiness theo-contextually means.
One cannot be holy, but not have been set apart by God, for only God can make one holy.
Thus, set apart by God and holy.

Either holy and righteous by God, or unholy and sinful apart from God.
Not holy and righteous by God.
Therefore, unholy and sinful apart from God.

SCRIPTURES

Leviticus 19:2—"Speak to all the congregation of the children of Israel, and say to them: 'You shall be holy, for I the Lord your God am holy.'"

Joshua 24:19—But Joshua said to the people, "You cannot serve the Lord, for He is a holy God. He is a jealous God; He will not forgive your transgressions nor your sins."

Isaiah 5:16—But the Lord of hosts shall be exalted in judgment, And God who is holy shall be hallowed in righteousness.

1 Peter 1:15-16—15 but as He who called you is holy, you also be holy in all your conduct, 16 because it is written, "Be holy, for I am holy."

1 Thessalonians 4:7-8—7 For God did not call us to uncleanness, but in holiness. 8 Therefore he who rejects this does not reject man, but God, who has also given us His Holy Spirit.

OBJECTIONS & RESPONSES

See "Transcendent," "Anthropology," and "Hamartiology" in conjunction with the above arguments in this section.

PRACTICAL POINTS TO PONDER

1. God is Unchanging Righteousness.
2. God's Righteousness remains unaffected by the affairs of the cosmos or the free moral agents who inhabit it (e.g., humans, angels, devils, etc.).
3. We can always count on God to do what is right, even when others do wrong.
4. We can count on God to save us from the penalty and power of sin, and set us apart to serve and worship Him.

OMNIBENEVOLENT

DEFINITION
God is all-good.

DESCRIPTION
God as "All-good" necessarily flows from His attributes of Infinity, Omnipotence, Omniscience, Immutability, Love, and Wisdom. God's Love is demonstrated in His unlimited and unchanging desire to do what is best for us. God's love for us is good, i.e., (the most) beneficial action that we can receive. In addition, God also has all knowledge, power, and unfailing ability to actualize, i.e., make come to pass, what is best for us. Therefore, in love, God is always able and willing to do for us that which most accords with His nature, i.e., that which is good, because God is good.

ARGUMENTS
God is perfect.
Perfect is without defect.
Without defect is good.
Thus, God is good.

God is Love.
Love is good.
God is Infinite.
Thus, God is Infinitely good, i.e., all-good.

Either God is all-good and will one day eradicate evil, or God is not all-good, or is impotent, or is malevolent and cannot eradicate evil.

But God is Infinite Love (non-malevolent) and Omnipotent. Thus, God is all-good and will one day eradicate evil.

SCRIPTURES

Psalm 34:8—Oh, taste and see that the Lord is good; Blessed is the man who trusts in Him!

Psalm 100:5—For the Lord is good; His mercy is everlasting, And His truth endures to all generations.

Jeremiah 33:11—Praise the Lord of hosts, For the Lord is good, For His mercy endures forever—and of those who will bring the sacrifice of praise into the house of the Lord.

Nahum 1:7—The Lord is good, A stronghold in the day of trouble; And He knows those who trust in Him.

1 John 4:16—And we have known and believed the love that God has for us. God is love, and he who abides in love abides in God, and God in him.

OBJECTIONS & RESPONSES

See "Omnipotent" and "Love."

PRACTICAL POINTS TO PONDER

1. God's goodness gives one hope in bad times.
2. God acts out of what God is. Since God is good, all of His acts are always for the good.
3. God alone is truly good. When one trusts God for the good, one can have an expectation to receive the ultimate good from God.

TRUTHFULNESS

DEFINITION

God is unchanging and ultimate reality.

DESCRIPTION

Truth is that which corresponds to reality. Reality is that which exists independently of all else. Therefore, "truth" is any real or realizable event, entity, statement, existence, etc., that resembles, agrees with, points to, indicates, or relates to actual independent existence. God is the only actual being that is Independent Being. Thus, God *is* Truth and thus the Source *of* Truth. All truth, then, will necessarily point back to God.

True "is what it is." To "tell the truth" is to "tell it like it is," as whatever it is corresponds to reality. God is Unchanging Existence, i.e., Reality. So whenever any truth claims are made, they are made with regard to the existing material (atoms, Adams, Eves, leaves, etc.) and non-material (thoughts, ideas, angels, etc.) universe established and sustained by God; such statements are also often made about God.

Since God exists, any claims made about any aspect of the universe should ultimately and accurately reflect the existence of the Creator and Sustainer of the universe, who is God. Also, any claims that obscure the true facts about the universe, of necessity, are a morally insulting to the very existence and nature of God.

ARGUMENTS

God is Pure Act.
Pure Act is Unchanging.
Unchanging is Eternal.
Eternal is Independent.
Independent is Reality.
Reality is Truth.
Thus, God is Truth.

If a thing corresponds to reality, then it is true.
A thing corresponds to reality.
Thus, a thing is true.

Either telling it like it is (which is truth), or telling it like it is not (which is telling a lie).
Not telling it like it is not.
Thus, telling it like it is.

SCRIPTURES

Jeremiah 10:10—But the Lord is the true God; he is the living God, the eternal King. When he is angry, the earth trembles; the nations cannot endure his wrath.

Isaiah 65:16—Whoever invokes a blessing in the land will do so by the one true God; whoever takes an oath in the land will swear by the one true God. For the past troubles will be forgotten and hidden from my eyes.

John 14:6—Jesus answered, "I am the way and the truth and the life. No one comes to the Father except through me."

John 15:26—"When the Advocate comes, whom I will send to you from the Father—the Spirit of truth who goes out from the Father—he will testify about me."

Romans 1:18-21—18 For the wrath of God is revealed from heaven against all ungodliness and unrighteousness of men, who suppress the truth in unrighteousness, 19 because what may be known of God is manifest in them, for God has shown it to them. 20 For since the creation of the world His invisible attributes are clearly seen, being understood by the things that are made, even His eternal power and Godhead, so that they are without excuse, 21 because, although they knew God, they did not glorify Him as God, nor were thankful, but became futile in their thoughts, and their foolish hearts were darkened.

1 John 5:20—We know also that the Son of God has come and has given us understanding, so that we may know him who is true. And we are in him who is true by being in his Son Jesus Christ. He is the true God and eternal life.

OBJECTIONS & RESPONSES

Objection 1: Truth does not Correspond to God

If truth equals reality, then God cannot equal truth since God does not correspond to Himself. This seems to be somewhat nonsensical.

Response 1: Truth does correspond to God

God is One, Simple, Perfect, Essential Being. God is only ever God. There is perfect correspondence of God with Himself. Therefore, God is truth.

NOTE: the same applies to Jesus Christ because Jesus Christ is also God (John 1:1-5, 14, 10:30, Colossians 2:9, etc.).

PRACTICAL POINTS TO PONDER
1. God alone is truly God and is Ultimate Reality.
2. God is unchanging, and thus can never be anything but Ultimate Reality, i.e., the truth.
3. God cannot and will not deceive you.
4. It is true that you can always trust the reality of God's unchanging love for you.

PERFECTION

DEFINITION

God has no defects in His nature or being.

DESCRIPTION

God's *Perfection* flows from His Pure Actuality, Aseity, and Necessity. God is simple, independent, self-existence with no potential to become anything other than what He essentially is. As such, God exists in and of Himself, meaning that God must also necessarily exist, because non-existence is an actual impossibility for God.

In that, God is also Eternal, Immutable, Immaterial, and Immortal. There is thus no possibility of defect, i.e., a lack of an essential / necessary or accidental / peripheral element of God's existence. There is no time when God is not God (Eternal); no possibility of change without time (Immutable); no atomic entity for change in time or space (Immaterial); and no possibility of cessation of existence (Immortal).

All of the above leads to God's Perfection in this: there is simply no way that God could ever not be God. Even so, by way of negation, one could arrive at the same conclusion via natural revelation.

Humans are not perfect because we are finite, mortal, dependent, temporal, changing, physical beings. All of those things are defects, or reveal an essential lack, in our existence, i.e., they are imperfections. And, in a moral sense, we clearly exhibit defectiveness in thought, word, and deed, often even against our own respective moral codes, let alone against God's holy commandments, which are written both upon our hearts and in the Bible (Romans 2:14-15).

We can look at our own imperfection—both individual and in the vast majority, maybe even totality, of humanity—and inductively reason to God's Perfection. Such a revelation will allow God's saving grace, through faith in Jesus Christ, to imbue us with His Perfection.

ARGUMENTS

God is Self-Existent.
What is Self-Existent is Independent.
What is Independent is Eternal.
What is Eternal is Immortal.
What is Immortal is Unlimited.
What is Unlimited is Immaterial.
What is Immaterial is Perfect.
Thus, God is Perfect.

If essentially Perfect and Immortal, then not imperfect and mortal.
Essentially Perfect and Immortal.
Thus, not imperfect and mortal.

Either God is the Perfect Self-Existent Source of all existence or God is something less than that or there is no God.
It is not the case that there is no God, for there must be an Uncaused Efficient and Sustaining Cause of all existing contingent entities.
Neither is it the case that God is less than the Perfect Self-Existent Source of all Existence because anything less than Self-Existence is a contingent entity, which means that it can lose some sense of its existential essence.
Thus, God is the Perfect Self-Existent Source of all existence.

Perfection

SCRIPTURES

Deuteronomy 32:4—He is the Rock, His work is perfect; For all His ways are justice, A God of truth and without injustice; Righteous and upright is He.

2 Samuel 22:31—As for God, His way is perfect; The word of the Lord is proven; He is a shield to all who trust in Him.

Matthew 5:48—Therefore you shall be perfect, just as your Father in heaven is perfect.

John 19:5-7—5 Then Jesus came out, wearing the crown of thorns and the purple robe. And Pilate said to them, "Behold the Man!" 6 Therefore, when the chief priests and officers saw Him, they cried out, saying, "Crucify Him, crucify Him!" Pilate said to them, "You take Him and crucify Him, for I find no fault in Him." 7 The Jews answered him, "We have a law, and according to our law He ought to die, because He made Himself the Son of God."

Romans 12:2—And do not be conformed to this world, but be transformed by the renewing of your mind, that you may prove what is that good and acceptable and perfect will of God.

OBJECTIONS & RESPONSES

Objection 1: We cannot know God's perfection.

If God is really the transcendent, infinite, eternal, and "all-whatever God" people say that God must be—and that those people clearly are not—then how can those same limited, temporal, time- and earth-bound people know that God is "perfect?" How could the "imperfect" conceive of "perfection?"

Response 1: One can apprehend a thing without comprehending a thing.

It is true that no mortal being or entity can comprehend the nature and essence of God, as analogically revealed in God's non-moral attributes and characteristics. However, free moral agents, i.e., human beings, can *apprehend* God's moral (shareable) attribute (God within Himself) of Perfection, if only by way of negation.

For example, one can view the cycle of seasons that occur throughout the course of the years. When observing nature, one can see that among nearly innumerable living things there is a time of renewal, growth, decline, then death (e.g., Spring, Summer, Fall, Winter). From this a person can easily surmise that these cycles continue without their intervention or engagement, and that they, too, will one day succumb to this same cycle. In that is the realization that there is an inherent lack (i.e., defect) in biological life—or any extant entity—to maintain or sustain its own existence. It is a reasonably unassailable assumption that time, circumstance, and decline will eventually overtake all finite and mortal things.

But since the existence of biological and non-biological entities has occurred; is occurring; and will likely continue to occur, then there must be a cause that is devoid of the inherent defect of non-life or non-existence, i.e., it does not and cannot change, nor cease to exist. It has the perfection of Self-Existence. That reasonable conclusion leads one to God as Perfect.

PRACTICAL POINTS TO PONDER

1. Human sin is the irrefutable evidence of imperfection in this world. It is the single greatest issue facing humanity.
2. Human imperfection cannot be overcome by human effort. This only leads to a life of futile frustrations and failings.
3. God's Perfection overcomes the imperfection of any human sin when one accepts His perfect plan for one's life: salvation by grace through faith in Jesus Christ.

JEALOUSY

DEFINITION

God vigorously defends His name and righteousness.

DESCRIPTION

Human jealousy typically involves the destructive, intense emotional desire for or against what someone else is or has. God's jealousy is a legitimate desire and zeal to defend His name and His righteousness. God does not desire what we are or what we have, because God created and sustains the entire universe. Neither is God against what we are or have because God is Self-Existent and Independent, not needing anything from anyone or anything else in order to be what and who He is.

However, God does desire that His name and actions are rightly attributed to Him, and that those which are untrue are not attributed to Him. In other words, God will not idly allow wickedness to be attributed to Him, neither will God allow His righteousness to be credited to others. God does, and always will, ardently and zealously defend His nature and character.

ARGUMENTS

If someone lies about someone else, then the liar has distorted reality.
Someone has lied about someone else.
Thus, the liar has distorted reality.

No Human should covet.
To covet is to be jealous of someone else.
Thus, no human should be jealous of someone else.

Either God is the Source of Truth and will always vigorously defend the truth, even about Himself, or God will arbitrarily allow untruth to go unpunished and undermine His Justice.

It is not the case that God allows untruth to go unpunished. God is merciful and allows free moral agents who propagate untruth to repent.

Neither is it the case that God undermines His own Justice. This is a logical and ontological impossibility because God cannot change (eternally Just) and thus cannot deny Himself.

Therefore, God is the Source of Truth and will always vigorously defend the truth (because God is unchangingly Just).

SCRIPTURES

Deuteronomy 5:7—You shall have no other gods before Me.

Deuteronomy 33:21—They have provoked Me to jealousy by what is not God; They have moved Me to anger by their foolish idols. But I will provoke them to jealousy by those who are not a nation; I will move them to anger by a foolish nation.

Exodus 34:13-14—13 But you shall destroy their altars, break their sacred pillars, and cut down their wooden images 14 (for you shall worship no other god, for the Lord, whose name is Jealous, is a jealous God).

1 Corinthians 10:19-21—19 What am I saying then? That an idol is anything, or what is offered to idols is anything? 20 Rather, that the things which the Gentiles sacrifice they sacrifice to demons and not to God, and I do not want you to have fellowship with demons. 21 You cannot drink the cup of the Lord and the cup of demons; you cannot

partake of the Lord's table and of the table of demons. 22 Or do we provoke the Lord to jealousy? Are we stronger than He?

Matthew 12:30-32—30 He who is not with Me is against Me, and he who does not gather with Me scatters abroad. 31 "Therefore I say to you, every sin and blasphemy will be forgiven men, but the blasphemy against the Spirit will not be forgiven men. 32 Anyone who speaks a word against the Son of Man, it will be forgiven him; but whoever speaks against the Holy Spirit, it will not be forgiven him, either in this age or in the age to come.

OBJECTIONS & RESPONSES

None noted. See also the above arguments in this section.

PRACTICAL POINTS TO PONDER

1. God does not punish sinful human actions out of pettiness or covetousness, but out of righteousness and love.
2. God's Mercy often allows opportunity for sinful human beings to repent.
3. God vigorously defends His righteous character. When God imputes the same to Believers in Christ, God will vigorously defend the same in Believers.

JUSTICE

DEFINITION

God gives each person what each person deserves.

DESCRIPTION

Usually when one thinks about "justice," one thinks in terms of the punishment of a person who may have done something wrong. However, with God *justice* is more than merely punishing a person for violating a law or some prescribed moral standard. Justice, also called *righteousness*, is within the very essence of God. With God, justice entails unfailingly giving each person what each person deserves according to what each person has done, whether good or evil. This "giving" is also called God's *distributive justice*.

In the case of doing what is good, God gives *rewards*. In the case of doing evil, God gives *punishments*. Because God is good, God cannot and will not punish one who does good as if one had done evil. Neither will God reward one for doing evil as if one had done good. God is Immutable Righteousness. He cannot change from what He is. God will always give good for good and bad for bad.

It is the case that God, from a human perspective, seems to *delay* punishing the bad (see "Mercy") or is *delinquent* in rewarding the good. However, God is Wise, Omniscient, and Omnipotent. God knows how to distribute Justice; the best way and time to distribute it; and has the power to execute it. In due season, God will reward the good and give retribution for the bad. God cannot fail in His Justice toward any free moral agents, whether humans, angels, or demons.

ARGUMENTS

If God rewards evil, then God cannot be all-Good.
But God is all-good.
Therefore, God does not reward evil.

God is Self-Existent.
Self-Existent is Infinite.
Infinite is Unlimited.
Unlimited is Immaterial.
Immaterial is Perfect.
Perfect is good.
Good is just.
Therefore, God is Just.

God is Self-Existent, Eternal, Omnipotent, Wise, and Good.
Thus, God can execute Justice at the right time, in all times, in all places, to all free moral agents.

SCRIPTURES

Job 34:12—Surely God will never do wickedly, Nor will the Almighty pervert justice.

Isaiah 30:18—Therefore the Lord will wait, that He may be gracious to you; And therefore He will be exalted, that He may have mercy on you. For the Lord is a God of justice; Blessed are all those who wait for Him.

Jeremiah 30:11—For I am with you,' says the Lord, 'to save you; Though I make a full end of all nations where I have scattered you, Yet I will not make a complete end of you. But I will correct you in justice, And will not let you go altogether unpunished.'

Romans 9:14—What shall we say then? Is there unrighteousness with God? Certainly not!

2 Corinthians 5:10—For we must all appear before the judgment seat of Christ, that each one may receive the things done in the body, according to what he has done, whether good or bad.

OBJECTIONS & RESPONSES

None noted. See also the above arguments in this section.

PRACTICAL POINTS TO PONDER
1. God rewards those who do what is good.
2. God punishes those who do what is evil.
3. In due season, God will give each one what each one is due.

WRATH

DEFINITION

God will punish all sin.

DESCRIPTION

Wrath is not merely God's unrestrained, uncontrolled, unmitigated anger at humanity's malevolent moral machinations against Him. Wrath is the realization of God's retribution against people's rejection of His grace, mercy, and love. It is God giving sinners what each sinner is due.

God is Just in executing wrath against sin because God is Love. God encourages and admonishes, but does not *force*, people to obey His commandments; forcing them to obey would be the opposite of love. God is also Good. His commandments for human beings *are* good and *for* their good.

Thus, God will not force human beings to accept or obey what is good for them. However, in rejecting what is good for them, they also reject God, the one who provided the good. In executing *retributive* justice via His Wrath, God gives each person what each one *deserves*, but also gives each one what each one *desires*: relational freedom from God's Love and Mercy.

ARGUMENTS

If one's sins are forgiven by grace through faith in Jesus Christ, then one is not subject to the wrath of God.
One's sins are forgiven by grace through faith in Jesus Christ.
Thus, one is not subject to the wrath of God.

Either subject to wrath or saved by grace and mercy.
Not subject to wrath.
Therefore, saved by grace and mercy.

If a person continually and unchangingly rejects God's love and mercy while living, then it would be unrighteous for God to reward that person with everlasting life in God's presence.
We know that many people have totally rejected and repudiated God's love and mercy, even up until the time they died.
Therefore, there should be no expectation that God would then make such people be with Him for eternity when they have clearly demonstrated when they were living on Earth that they did not want to be with God.

SCRIPTURES

2 Chronicles 36:15-16—15 And the Lord God of their fathers sent warnings to them by His messengers, rising up early and sending them, because He had compassion on His people and on His dwelling place. 16 But they mocked the messengers of God, despised His words, and scoffed at His prophets, until the wrath of the Lord arose against His people, till there was no remedy.

Nahum 1:2—God is jealous, and the Lord avenges; The Lord avenges and is furious. The Lord will take vengeance on His adversaries.

Romans 1:18-20—18 For the wrath of God is revealed from heaven against all ungodliness and unrighteousness of men, who suppress the truth in unrighteousness, 19 because what may be known of God is manifest in them, for God has shown it to them. 20 For since the creation of the world His invisible attributes are clearly seen, being understood by the things that are made, even His eternal power and Godhead, so that they are without excuse.

Colossians 3:5-7—5 Therefore put to death your members which are on the earth: fornication, uncleanness, passion, evil desire, and covetousness, which is idolatry. 6 Because of these things the wrath of God is coming upon the sons of disobedience, 7 in which you yourselves once walked when you lived in them.

1 Thessalonians 5:5-9—5 You are all sons of light and sons of the day. We are not of the night nor of darkness. 6 Therefore let us not sleep, as others do, but let us watch and be sober. 7 For those who sleep, sleep at night, and those who get drunk are drunk at night. 8 But let us who are of the day be sober, putting on the breastplate of faith and love, and as a helmet the hope of salvation. 9 For God did not appoint us to wrath, but to obtain salvation through our Lord Jesus Christ.

OBJECTIONS & RESPONSES

Objection 1: God is unjust is punishing sin.

Since God created human beings with the ability to sin, then how can God be angry when they sin? Isn't God just being angry with Himself for not doing a good job in creating humans? Or is it the case that God is hypocritical because He wants them to accept Him like He is, but He doesn't accept them like they are? God is wrong for punishing people for their sins.

Response 1: God is not unjust in punishing sin.

God endowed humankind with free will. To argue to the contrary is a self-defeating argument against that fact. Human beings are able to make free choices in that 1) we are able to do what we are ontologically able to do, and 2) we can become what we are ontologically able to become.

No mortal human being can, by mere or sheer free will, do all that God can do because no mortal human being is God (Note: Jesus is the God-Man). No human being can, by mere free will, existentially and ontologically become something non-human (e.g., a rock or a whale).

However, human beings can make free moral choices. Sin is the free moral choice to do what God has *not* commanded or to not do what God *has* commanded. In either case, God offers a choice to remain bound by sin and thus condemned, or to be forgiven for sin and thus saved from sin's penalty, death. The choice is within the realm of human nature (i.e., via free will) and couched in God's Love and Mercy. Acceptance of God's forgiveness leads to blessed life in relationship with God, and that, everlasting life. Rejection of God's forgiveness leads to wretched death (i.e., eternal relational separation from God), and that everlasting.

God does accept us as He made us: very good (Genesis 1:31). However, very good is not Perfect. Yet, God offers perfection to humankind through His salvation plan in Christ Jesus. God is not wrong in punishing sin. God is just in giving unrepentant sinners what sinners desire and deserve: eternal freedom from God's prescriptions, proscriptions, and comforting presence.

PRACTICAL POINTS TO PONDER

1. Evil will not eternally prevail.
2. God's wrath will one day be revealed and executed against all sin.
3. Those who are in Christ Jesus have not been appointed to wrath, but to salvation and everlasting life.

MERCY

DEFINITION

God is love, which tempers His punishment of sin.

DESCRIPTION

Mercy is God's unfailing ability to not immediately punish humans every time they sin, but to allow humans an opportunity to repent and be restored to fellowship with Him. This is a natural concomitant of God's love, or God as Love, wherein God is always desirous of the best outcome for our lives. God's Mercy is also related to His Wrath and Justice. God's Justice is to grant to each one according to what each one has done: good for good, and bad for bad. Mercy comes in when humans sin, but God does not require immediate payment or recompense for it, i.e., have to experience God's Wrath.

This does *not* mean that God is pleased with sin, sanctions sin, causes sin, or allows sin to go unpunished. This *does* mean that humans are often the undeserving, unqualified beneficiaries of God's love at all times. God is the Source of Life. God desires most that which is most like Him. God does not desire that humans die for their sins, but that all would choose life that He lovingly provides.

Mercy is the key that unlocks the door for humans to repent from their sins and accept God's gracious gift of life.

ARGUMENTS

If loving, then merciful.
Loving.

Therefore, merciful.

Either God punishes all sin at all times, or God encourages sin. It is not the case that God encourages sin. Sin is to disobey God; fall short of His standard; or miss the mark that God has set. For God to encourage sin would be for God to deny His own Righteousness, which is impossible since God cannot deny Himself (i.e., is Immutable).
Neither is it the case that God punishes all sin at all times. People can clearly see that they themselves or others sin, but that sin is not always immediately punished.
Since neither case is true, God's Mercy is the answer: it allows sinners a chance to repent before God executes His retribution against their sin.

The wages of sin is death.
Death can be delayed through God's Mercy.
Thus, the wages of sin can be delayed through God's Mercy.

SCRIPTURES

Exodus 15:13—You in Your mercy have led forth The people whom You have redeemed; You have guided them in Your strength To Your holy habitation.

Nehemiah 1:5—And I said: "I pray, Lord God of heaven, O great and awesome God, You who keep Your covenant and mercy with those who love You and observe Your commandments."

Lamentations 3:22-24—22 Through the Lord's mercies we are not consumed, Because His compassions fail not. 23 They are new every morning; Great is Your faithfulness. 24 "The Lord is my portion," says my soul, "Therefore I hope in Him!"

Matthew 9:13—"But go and learn what this means: 'I desire mercy and not sacrifice.' For I did not come to call the righteous, but sinners, to repentance."

Matthew 5:7—Blessed are the merciful, For they shall obtain mercy.

OBJECTIONS & RESPONSES

Objection 1: God's Mercy encourages sinful actions.

If God is always unchangingly, infinitely, eternally, jealously righteous and good, then there should be no time at all that God allows human sin to go unpunished. However, it is clear that there is incalculably gross and rampant sin in the world that is clearly going unpunished. It is evident that God's inaction against sin, i.e., "mercy," encourages more sin.

Response 1: God's Mercy reveals love towards sinful actors.

God is Immutable, Infinite, Eternal, Jealous, and Just. In all of those things, God is also Love. God's Love does not change; is limitless; is timeless; and definitive of His character, which is to seek the good of—even the best for—humankind. Just because God's love allows room for humans to repent of sin does not mean that God encourages sin. That would be for God to encourage that which is against His nature, which God cannot and will not do. Mercy should be viewed in the light of God's *essence*: it is everlasting; however, humanity is not. Though God's Mercy may allow sinful actions to occur for a time, eventually—according to His knowledge, plan, and purpose for such persons—Mercy will no longer avail and righteous retribution will prevail (see "Wrath").

PRACTICAL POINTS TO PONDER

1. God is not on immediately punishing every instance of sin that you may commit.
2. God is love, and desires that you repent from sin and live.
3. Whenever sin manifests—whether knowingly or unwittingly, via commission or omission—do not be fettered by guilt, but free through repentant confession to God of your sin.

ANTHROPOLOGY

DEFINITION

Christian Anthropology is the study of humanity's nature from a Christian perspective.

DESCRIPTION

Among many significant attributes, human beings are, most notably, mortal, finite, dependent, and temporal beings. Humans are born in space-time, but have a duality of nature that is simultaneously material and immaterial, yet distinct, i.e., each nature is of a different essence than the other. This can also be referred to as a unified dichotomy of essence, or as *hylomorphism* (Geisler, *Systematic Vol. 3*, 66-69).

Humans have the ability to transcend their limited state by virtue of their abilities to imagine and to reason. Humans can and do make rational choices among real alternatives. This is also referred to as humans having the free will to select among real and / or realizable options.

Human beings are most basically and naturally able to create other human beings after their kind (species) by virtue of coital engagement between an actual, biological male and a biological female, i.e., intergender procreative copulation.

Human beings are relational beings, within the respective contexts of the cosmos—other human beings, other sentient and / or non-sentient life, non-human beings—and God. Often, there is reciprocity of relationship between humans and the aforementioned relational entities wherein any or all have some discernible impact on the other.

According to the Bible, every human is made in the image and after the likeness of God, and given dominion over non-human creation (Genesis 1:26-27). In a rational biblical, theological, and philosophical context, this means that human beings share in God's non-corporeal (spiritual) moral essence, e.g., the ability love, do good things, be truthful, exercise authority, demonstrate justice, and mercy, etc. And with those moral attributes and characteristics is the expectation—sometimes implicit (natural revelation) or explicit (the Holy Bible)—that human beings should exercise sound judgment and wisdom in their autonomous fiat relational stewardship of creation, as God clearly prescribes and directs.

ARGUMENTS

If mortal, then human.
Mortal.
Therefore, human.

Either caused and human or uncaused and God.
Not uncaused and God.
Thus, caused and human.

Human beings are finite.
Finite is limited.
Limited is imperfect.
Imperfect is lacking.
Lacking is temporal.
Temporal is dependent.
Dependent is contingent.
Contingent is to need an Uncaused Actualizing and Sustaining Cause.

Thus, human beings need an Uncaused Actualizing Sustaining Cause.

SCRIPTURES

Genesis 1:26-28—26 Then God said, "Let Us make man in Our image, according to Our likeness; let them have dominion over the fish of the sea, over the birds of the air, and over the cattle, over all the earth and over every creeping thing that creeps on the earth." 27 So God created man in His own image; in the image of God He created him; male and female He created them. 28 Then God blessed them, and God said to them, "Be fruitful and multiply; fill the earth and subdue it; have dominion over the fish of the sea, over the birds of the air, and over every living thing that moves on the earth."

Genesis 5:2—He created them male and female, and blessed them and called them Mankind in the day they were created.

Psalm 8:4-6—4 What is man that You are mindful of him, And the son of man that You visit him? 5 For You have made him a little lower than the angels, And You have crowned him with glory and honor. 6 You have made him to have dominion over the works of Your hands; You have put all things under his feet.

Mark 10:6-8—6 But from the beginning of the creation, God 'made them male and female.' 7 'For this reason a man shall leave his father and mother and be joined to his wife, 8 and the two shall become one flesh'; so then they are no longer two, but one flesh.

Acts 17:26-28—26 And He has made from one blood every nation of men to dwell on all the face of the earth, and has determined their preappointed times and the boundaries of their dwellings, 27 so that they should seek the Lord, in the hope that they might grope for Him and find Him, though He is not far from each one of us; 28 for in Him we live and move and have our being, as also some of your own poets have said, 'For we are also His offspring.'

OBJECTIONS & RESPONSES

None noted. See also the above arguments in this section.

PRACTICAL POINTS TO PONDER

1. Every human being has great worth and value because every human is like, and comes from, God.
2. Human beings have fiat authority from God to exercise wise authority over the earth.
3. Human beings can exercise free will among real and realizable alternatives, the most important of which is about their reciprocal relationship with Creator God.

BIBLIOLOGY

DEFINITION

Bibliology is the study of the Bible.

DESCRIPTION

The Bible is a holy book from God, mediated to humankind over the course of several millennia through approximately 40 human writers. The Protestant Bible has 66 canonical books written in at least nine different genres. It is divided into two distinct Testaments: Old, containing 39 books, and New, containing 27 books. The Bible is written in three distinct languages: Hebrew and Aramaic (Old Testament), and Koine Greek (New Testament). The Bible internally self-identifies as the Word of God, but also has internal and external evidence of being historically accurate. To date, it is the definitive and most reliable source about the life, person, purpose, power, plan, and provision of Jesus Christ.

The *Efficient* cause of the Bible is God, who used human beings as *Instrumental* causes to record and capture only that which God wanted them to record and capture. That essentially entails both *verbal* (God-spoken) and *plenary* (God-directed) inspiration of the Bible. Though written via human agency, the Bible has no errors in the original writings, called the *autographa* (not known to be in existence), and no material errors in the copies from which translations come today (thousands of various copies in existence).

The Bible is highly useful for moral guidance in understanding things about God, humankind, the current world or age in which we live, and the future destiny for humankind and the remaining cosmos.

ARGUMENTS

God cannot err.
The Bible comes from God.
Thus, the Bible cannot err.

If passing rigorous tests for truth, then reliable.
The Bible has passed rigorous tests for truth.
Therefore, the Bible is reliable.

Either the Holy Bible as it exists today is trustworthy concerning reality, or it is untrustworthy concerning reality, or there is another source about reality that is more trustworthy.
It is not the case that the Bible is untrustworthy concerning reality, for there are many texts within the Bible that accurately describe many significant aspects of reality and prescribe human moral actions according to reality.
Neither is it the case that some other source supersedes the Bible in accurately describing significant aspects of reality, for 1) the Bible, as it is today, carries many substantial earmarks and proofs (historically, philosophically, realistically) as having come from God, and 2) the Bible has withstood many attempts at terminal refutation through the millennia, yet remains intact today as a trustworthy source of truth for billions of people.
Therefore, the Holy Bible as it exists today is trustworthy concerning reality.

Bibliology

SCRIPTURES

Deuteronomy 6:4-7—4 "Hear, O Israel: The Lord our God, the Lord is one! 5 You shall love the Lord your God with all your heart, with all your soul, and with all your strength. 6 "And these words which I command you today shall be in your heart. 7 You shall teach them diligently to your children, and shall talk of them when you sit in your house, when you walk by the way, when you lie down, and when you rise up."

Deuteronomy 29:29—The secret things belong to the Lord our God, but those things which are revealed belong to us and to our children forever, that we may do all the words of this law.

Psalm 119:11—Your word I have hidden in my heart, That I might not sin against You.

Psalm 119:105—Your word is a lamp to my feet and a light to my path.

1 Peter 2:19-21—19 And so we have the prophetic word confirmed, which you do well to heed as a light that shines in a dark place, until the day dawns and the morning star rises in your hearts; 20 knowing this first, that no prophecy of Scripture is of any private interpretation, 21 for prophecy never came by the will of man, but holy men of God spoke as they were moved by the Holy Spirit.

OBJECTIONS & RESPONSES

Objection 1: The original Bible manuscripts do not exist; therefore, the copies are unreliable.

It is freely admitted by ardent adherents of the Bible that the "original" writings are no longer in existence. But if the original writings are no longer in existence, then there is no baseline to which the existing copies—from which the current Bible translations come—can be compared. Therefore, there is no way to prove the reliability of the current copies, which then questions the Bible's historical and literal accuracy.

Response 1: The existing copies are reliable and trustworthy.

Although the original Bible manuscripts are not known to be in existence today, myriads of copies do exist. The importance of this is that 1) if the autographa were extant today, they would likely be subject to maleficent manipulation by malignant malefactors of free moral agency, and 2) the copies serve as a clear buffer that detects possible manipulation while facilitating comparative accuracy to the autographa. In other words, the existence of many copies does not call into question the accuracy of the current Bible translations, but instead helps to confirm the accuracy.

In addition, many significant studies and empirical efforts have been undertaken through the years regarding the relative historical and grammatical accuracy of the current Bible translations. Suffice it to say, there is at least 98+% agreement between known Bible manuscripts (up to 99.9+%), and any discrepancies affect no contextual understanding nor points of Christian doctrine, thus proving immaterial. The existing copies are remarkably reliable and trustworthy.

Objection 2: The Bible does have errors. Therefore, the Bible is untrustworthy.

Bibliology

Any reasonable Bible believer would freely admit that the current Bible translations have discrepancies in them. This is clearly evident in the many "study Bibles" that have footnotes denoting such things. Since that is an undeniable fact, it is undeniable that the Bible has errors in it, and is therefore untrustworthy.

Response 2: The current Bible translations have no material errors. Therefore, the current Bible translations are trustworthy.

This objection is similar to *Objection 1* above, with the exception that this argument attacks the *results* of the manuscripts, i.e., the current Bible translations. It is also the informal logical fallacy called the "Genetic Fallacy" (i.e., reject this because of its origins) or an *ad hominem circumstantial* fallacy (i.e., reject this because it is associated with something considered bad or deficient, etc.; Geisler, *Come*). In either case, the Bible's trustworthiness is not harmed. Recall from "Objection 1" that the copies are at least 98+% in agreement with one another, and the remaining differences are immaterial relative to one's understanding of what is written and points of Christian doctrine. Thus, the current translations are free from material errors and are trustworthy.

PRACTICAL POINTS TO PONDER

1. You can trust that the Bible will give you invaluable truth about reality as it is.
2. You can trust that the Bible is reliable in the things that it purports to be true.
3. You can trust that the Bible has been given by God to humankind so that we can understand (*apprehend*) His nature, our nature, and the nature of all significant aspects of life, both now and in the future.

HAMARTIOLOGY

DEFINITION

Hamartiology is the study of sin committed by free moral agents.

DESCRIPTION

Sin is the deliberate breach of a legitimate moral standard. It is "missing the mark" of moral perfection. It is to "go beyond" prescribed boundaries. It is "all the bad things we do." Ultimately, sin is the state in which free moral agents fail to obey God's holy commandments.

Sin occurs via *action* or *inaction*, e.g., *doing* what is wrong or *not* doing what is right. Sin is also realized in one's thinking, i.e., wishing ill upon someone else or oneself, or meditatively musing upon some form of malfeasance that is contrary to the revealed moral code of God.

This moral code is innate to every human being, as understood in the general concept of "right" and its antithesis, i.e., "not-right" (wrong, bad, evil, etc.). God's moral *prescriptions* ("*should* do") and *proscriptions* ("should *not* do") are also revealed in the Bible. The Bible is God's self-disclosure to humankind so that we can understand more about Him, ourselves, and the world that was, is, and is to come.

Since what God expects from humankind in a moral sense is innate to us, and expressly stated in the Bible, humankind is without excuse relative to its knowledge of God's moral expectations. Human beings

Hamartiology

too often simply reject God's moral code. That rejection is sin: the exercise of human free will against the will of God.

Sin's existence as a result of wayward human will has doubtless caused great ill, disunity, destruction, degradation of soul, and death among the denizens of this world in days past; today; and likely in the days to come. Still, it is as comforting to know that God *forgives* sin as it is also, perhaps, distressing to know that God also *punishes* sin.

(See "Justice," "Mercy," "Wrath," "Holiness," and "Eschatology" for more.)

ARGUMENTS

Humans are free moral agents.
Sin is committed by free moral agents.
Thus, sin is committed by humans.

If in breach of a moral code, then a sin-committer.
In breach of a moral code.
Therefore, a sin-committer.

Either a person is sin-free and not in breach of God's moral code, or a person commits sins and breaks God's moral code.
A person breaks God's moral code.
Thus, a person is not sin-free and commits sins, breaking God's moral code (i.e., is a sinner).

SCRIPTURES

Genesis 2:15-17—15 Then the Lord God took the man and put him in the garden of Eden to tend and keep it. 16 And the Lord God commanded the man, saying, "Of every tree of the garden you may freely eat; 17 but of the tree of the knowledge of good and evil you shall not eat, for in the day that you eat of it you shall surely die."

Genesis 3:9-11—9 Then the Lord God called to Adam and said to him, "Where are you?" 10 So he said, "I heard Your voice in the garden, and I was afraid because I was naked; and I hid myself." 11 And He said, "Who told you that you were naked? Have you eaten from the tree of which I commanded you that you should not eat?"

Genesis 4:6-8—6 So the Lord said to Cain, "Why are you angry? And why has your countenance fallen? 7 If you do well, will you not be accepted? And if you do not do well, sin lies at the door. And its desire is for you, but you should rule over it." 8 Now Cain talked with Abel his brother; and it came to pass, when they were in the field, that Cain rose up against Abel his brother and killed him.

Romans 3:23—For all have sinned and fall short of the glory of God.

Romans 6:23—For the wages of sin is death, but the gift of God is eternal life in Christ Jesus our Lord.

1 John 8:8-10—8 If we say that we have no sin, we deceive ourselves, and the truth is not in us. 9 If we confess our sins, He is faithful and just to forgive us our sins and to cleanse us from all unrighteousness. 10 If we say that we have not sinned, we make Him a liar, and His word is not in us.

OBJECTIONS & RESPONSES

Objection 1: God lets people sin when it suits him.

In the Bible, God seems to sanction and subsequently reward a woman, Rahab, for lying to conceal the whereabouts of Jewish spies

(Joshua Chapter 2, and Chapter 6, verses 22-23). Another time, in 1 Kings 22:19-23, God allowed a spirit-being of some sort to be a "lying spirit" to some prophets. In both cases, God lets sin occur when it seems to suit him.

Response 1: God uses all means at His disposal to accomplish His ends.

In response to this objection, there is an *explication* about the character of God and an *implication* about the character of free moral agents that must be clarified in order to understand the fact that God does not allow sin merely when it suits Him.

First and foremost, God cannot and does not lie. God is Immutable, Truthful, Just, and Holy. Thus, God's character is reasonably unassailable with regard to the sin of lying. There is also the implication that both Rahab and the "lying spirit," as free moral agents (one a human being, the other a spirit-being) were themselves unaffected by sin.

Rahab appears to have been a woman of questionable character living among a people upon whom God's retributive judgment had clearly fallen. She knew this, and sought self-preservation through lying. God simply used her bad moral state to accomplish a good outcome: the safety of His people in surveying the land (and the preservation of life to a woman—and her family—who recognized God's power and people).

The "lying spirit" account occurs within the context of a vision from the prophet Micaiah, a true prophet of God. In it, God accepts the proposal of the spirit-being to continue deceiving those who had clearly and consistently rejected the truth that God had sent through His written word (the Law) and spoken word (via the prophets). Thus, God did not act as the Efficient Cause of the "lying spirit" within the vision, but used the willful spirit to accomplish the Final Cause of the destruction of a wicked and rebellious king, Ahab.

Therefore, in neither case is it true that God lets people sin when it suits Him, with the implication that God is the cause of such sin.

PRACTICAL POINTS TO PONDER

1. Sin is the breach by free moral agents (i.e., human and spirit beings) of God's clearly revealed moral code.
2. Sin occurs via action or inaction, and also in one's thinking.
3. The result of sin is continued discord, disharmony, contention, and chaos among human beings . . . and ultimately, destruction of those who continue to do it.

CHRISTOLOGY

DEFINITION

Christology is the study of God the Son, the Lord Jesus Christ.

DESCRIPTION

Understanding the meaning of the following words is key to understanding Christology. They are:

Lord: "one who has authority."
Jesus: "God saves."
Christ: "anointed or chosen one."

Thus, Christology is the study of the Lord Jesus Christ as the One chosen to wield the authority to save humankind.

Human beings are free moral agents who can freely choose to obey or disobey God. God rewards obedience and punishes disobedience. Jesus Christ, who is God the Son and the Son of God (see "Unity," "Triunity," and "Simplicity") came to Earth to be a substitutionary sacrifice for the sins of all humankind (see "Soteriology"). The totality of the life of Jesus was that all who believe in Him as the Son of God—and Savior of humankind, also called "Messiah"—could have their sins forgiven and receive eternal life.

According to the Holy Scriptures, Jesus willingly came from Heaven down to Earth, via the mechanism of a miraculous birth (genetic material from Mary, but none from a human father) to save fallen humankind. He was "Immanuel," meaning "God with us." As such,

Jesus performed many miracles (e.g., healing the sick; raising the dead to life; exhibiting control over nature, etc.) and gave other proofs (e.g., fulfillment of prophecies, great wisdom in teaching) to the people of His day. He did this so that they would accept the true testimony about who He was, and what He was there to do then and in the future: save the repentant humanity from the penalty of its sins.

Jesus prophesied His own death and resurrection, both of which historically occurred. He also made a promise to all who believed in Him as the Son of God and Savior that He would one day return for them, and that as He was—resurrected from physical death to everlasting life with an imperishable, uncorruptible body—so they would also be. He would be with them—and they with Him—forever.

ARGUMENTS

The Bible says that God created the cosmos.
The Bible says that Jesus created the cosmos.
The Bible says that Jesus and the Father are "one."
The Bible says that Jesus is the Son of God.
Thus, it is clear from the Bible that Jesus is God the Son.

If one fulfills predictive prophecies about being the Savior of humanity, then one is the Savior of humanity.
Jesus fulfills predictive prophecies about being the Savior of humanity.
Therefore, Jesus is the Savior of humanity.

Either Jesus displayed evidence for being the Savior of humanity, or Jesus provided no proof of being humanity's Savior.
It is not the case that Jesus provided no proof of being humanity's Savior.
Thus, Jesus displayed evidence for being the Savior of humanity.

SCRIPTURES

Genesis 1:1—In the beginning God created the heavens and the earth.

John 1:1-3—In the beginning was the Word, and the Word was with God, and the Word was God. 2 He was in the beginning with God. 3 All things were made through Him, and without Him nothing was made that was made.

Isaiah 9:6—6 For unto us a Child is born, Unto us a Son is given; And the government will be upon His shoulder. And His name will be called Wonderful, Counselor, Mighty God, Everlasting Father, Prince of Peace.

John 10:30-33—30 I and My Father are one." 31 Then the Jews took up stones again to stone Him. 32 Jesus answered them, "Many good works I have shown you from My Father. For which of those works do you stone Me?" 33 The Jews answered Him, saying, "For a good work we do not stone You, but for blasphemy, and because You, being a Man, make Yourself God."

John 3:14-18—14 And as Moses lifted up the serpent in the wilderness, even so must the Son of Man be lifted up, 15 that whoever believes in Him should not perish but have eternal life. 16 For God so loved the world that He gave His only begotten Son, that whoever believes in Him should not perish but have everlasting life. 17 For God did not send His Son into the world to condemn the world, but that the world through Him might be saved. 18 "He who believes in Him is not condemned; but he who does not believe is condemned already, because he has not believed in the name of the only begotten Son of God.

OBJECTIONS & RESPONSES

See "Eternal," "Immense," "Immortal," "Immutable," "Impassible," "Infinite," "Life," and "Simple."

PRACTICAL POINTS TO PONDER

1. The historical Jesus actually lived.
2. The historical Jesus actually came from Heaven to Earth and dwelt among humankind.
3. The historical Jesus actually died and resurrected back to life to fulfill His promise to save any human being who believes in Him as the Son of God.
4. Jesus will keep His promise to return for all who believe in Him for salvation, rescuing them from God's wrath against this world's sins; then they will be with Jesus forever.

SOTERIOLOGY

DEFINITION

Soteriology is the study of salvation.

DESCRIPTION

Salvation, in the greatest sense, is the satisfaction of a debt owed, and the resulting state of being justified in the sight of the one to whom the debt was owed. It is to redeem or to purchase one from the possession of another because of such a debt. In that vein, a biblical soteriology begins with the Fall of humankind by the free moral choices of its progenitors, Adam and Eve, but ends with the redemption of any individual person, by God's grace, through faith, in Jesus Christ (see "Christology").

According to the Holy Bible in Genesis Chapters Two and Three, the man and the woman were each given a single commandment by God to obey, which they each clearly understood, and were also given a promise of retribution if that commandment was broken. When the choice was individually made by each to disregard and disobey God's singular command to not eat of the fruit from the Tree of the Knowledge of Good and Evil, God's Justice was realized and distributed: death. Death entered this world because of their antecedent act of sin. From that point on, neither one of them, nor anyone else, could stand before God as being "just" or "righteous."

However, it is important to note that God's promise of life and salvation were yet in place from eternity, as revealed in the Holy Bible, since 1) salvation for humankind was prophesied by God in

Genesis 3:15 ("And I will put enmity Between you and the woman, And between your seed and her Seed; He shall bruise your head, And you shall bruise His heel") and reassured in Galatians 3:16 ("Now to Abraham and his Seed were the promises made. He does not say, "And to seeds," as of many, but as of one, "And to your Seed," who is Christ), and 2) life even after the Fall was granted to Adam, Eve, and their progeny (see Genesis 3:16-20).

The salvation of humankind was, and is, necessary due to the imputed sin from Adam and Eve, and the subsequent inability of those born of two human parents to not sin against God (Jesus had only one human parent, the virgin Mary). No one was able to pay the debt owed to an Infinite, Eternal, Holy, and Just God. However, that same God, who is also loving and merciful in the same aforementioned ways, took it upon Himself to satisfy the sin debt for us. The death of Jesus Christ satisfied the sin debt. His resurrection secured salvation for all who would believe.

Syntactically, grammatically, and theologically, once a person believes that Jesus is the Son of God and Savior, i.e., is saved, that person is saved once and for all. There is no real possibility of one becoming unjustified. Salvation is offered to temporal people, but secured by the Eternal God. In salvation, the relational breach between God and any individual is closed; the door to reconciliation remains open; and the possibility of loving, lasting, eternal relationship with Creator God can be realized, both now and in eternity.

ARGUMENTS

Human beings sin.
Sin leads to death.
Death can be averted by God's Mercy.

God's Mercy allows God's Grace.
God's Grace makes salvation available to humans, through their individual faith.
Thus, human beings can be saved by God's grace, through their faith.

If sinful or unforgiven, then in need of salvation.
Sinful.
Therefore, in need of salvation.

Either justified by grace through faith and not subject to eternal punishment, or unjustified by no grace nor faith and subject to eternal punishment.
One is not justified by grace through faith.
Therefore, one is unjustified by no grace nor faith and subject to eternal punishment.

SCRIPTURES

1 Chronicles 16:34-35—34 Oh, give thanks to the Lord, for He is good! For His mercy endures forever. 35 And say, "Save us, O God of our salvation; Gather us together, and deliver us from the Gentiles, To give thanks to Your holy name, To triumph in Your praise."

John 3:36—He who believes in the Son has everlasting life; and he who does not believe the Son shall not see life, but the wrath of God abides on him.

John 5:24—Most assuredly, I say to you, he who hears My word and believes in Him who sent Me has everlasting life, and shall not come into judgment, but has passed from death into life.

Romans 5:12, 17— 12 Therefore, just as through one man sin entered the world, and death through sin, and thus death spread to all men, because all sinned . . . 17 For if by the one man's offense death reigned through the one, much more those who receive abundance of grace and of the gift of righteousness will reign in life through the One, Jesus Christ.

1 John 1:6-9—6 If we say that we have fellowship with Him, and walk in darkness, we lie and do not practice the truth. 7 But if we walk in the light as He is in the light, we have fellowship with one another, and the blood of Jesus Christ His Son cleanses us from all sin. 8 If we say that we have no sin, we deceive ourselves, and the truth is not in us. 9 If we confess our sins, He is faithful and just to forgive us our sins and to cleanse us from all unrighteousness.

OBJECTIONS & RESPONSES

See "Mercy," "Hamartiology," and "Wrath."

PRACTICAL POINTS TO PONDER

1. Sin entered the world through Adam, but salvation entered the world through Jesus Christ.
2. God takes no pleasure in the death of anyone who dies, but greatly desires that all live.
3. Receiving God's gift of salvation, by grace through faith in Jesus Christ, secures one's justification for all time.

PNEUMATOLOGY

DEFINITION

Pneumatology is the study of God the Holy Spirit.

DESCRIPTION

The Holy Spirit is one of the three Eternal "Who's" in the Triune "What" that is God. The Holy Spirit is a non-incarnate Person of the Triune Godhead (unlike God the Son, who added human nature and became the incarnate "Immanuel"), but is one who dwells within those who believe in Jesus Christ as the Son of God.

Although the Holy Spirit can empower human beings, the Holy Spirit is not merely the extension of God's actualized power, e.g., like a battery to a toy or electric current from an outlet to a device. The Holy Spirit demonstrates all of the characteristics of personhood and is able to non-corporeally and immaterially—yet causally and effectively—live *within* a Christian (and the Scriptures show that He can be *upon* non-Christians) to act in myriad ways. Some of the characteristics and actions of the Holy Spirit are as follow:

- Leads / guides (John 16:13; Romans 8:14; Galatians 5:16, 18)
- Empowers (Exodus 31:1-5, 35:30-35; Zechariah 4:6-8; Mic. 3:8; Acts 1:8)
- Indwells (John 14:16-17)
- Fills (Luke 1:15, 41, 67; Acts 9:17, 13:8-10)
- Gives hope (Romans 15:13)
- Sanctifies (Romans 15:16)
- Gives gifts (Hebrews 2:4)

- Provides fellowship (2 Corinthians 13:14)
- Also teaches (Nehemiah 9:20; John 14:26), commands (Acts 8:29, 13:2-3), convicts (John 16:8); intercedes for (Romans 8:26), and commissions believers (Acts 13:4)

Given those attributes and actions, the Holy Spirit is clearly not merely inanimate, mindless power, neither an impersonal force used by God the Father, nor just a subordinate entity sent by Jesus. The Holy Spirit is, in fact and from all eternity, God. This is as also evidenced by the following titles revealed in Scripture:

- Spirit of God (Numbers 24:2, Rom. 8:9, 14)
- Spirit of the Lord (Judges 3:10, 2 Corinthians 3:17)
- Spirit of the Father (Matthew 10:20)
- Spirit of Jesus (Acts 16:7)
- Spirit of Christ (Romans 8:9)
- Spirit of the Son (Galatians 4:6)
- Spirit of Truth (John 15:26, 16:12-14)

ARGUMENTS

God is Eternal and God has thoughts.
Thoughts only occur within a mind.
Thus, God's Eternal thoughts come from God's Eternal Mind.
Eternal is also timeless, which means unlimited, which means Infinite.
The Holy Spirit knows God's Eternal, Infinite thoughts.
But only Eternal and Infinite can know the same.
Thus, the Holy Spirit is Eternal and Infinite, i.e., the Holy Spirit is God.

God is Truth.
The Bible calls the Holy Spirit the "Spirit of Truth."
Therefore, the Holy Spirit is God.

The Bible clearly shows that at least Three Persons are God.
The Holy Spirit is one of those Three.
Therefore, the Holy Spirit is God.

SCRIPTURES

Genesis 1:2—The earth was without form, and void; and darkness was on the face of the deep. And the Spirit of God was hovering over the face of the waters.

Isaiah 63:9-11—9 In all their affliction He was afflicted, And the Angel of His Presence saved them; In His love and in His pity He redeemed them; And He bore them and carried them All the days of old. 10 But they rebelled and grieved His Holy Spirit; So He turned Himself against them as an enemy, And He fought against them. 11 Then he remembered the days of old, Moses and his people, saying: "Where is He who brought them up out of the sea With the shepherd of His flock? Where is He who put His Holy Spirit within them . . .

John 14:26—26 But the Helper, the Holy Spirit, whom the Father will send in My name, He will teach you all things, and bring to your remembrance all things that I said to you.

John 16:13—13 However, when He, the Spirit of truth, has come, He will guide you into all truth; for He will not speak on His own authority, but whatever He hears He will speak; and He will tell you things to come.

Romans 8:8-10—8 So then, those who are in the flesh cannot please God. 9 But you are not in the flesh but in the Spirit, if indeed the Spirit of God dwells in you. Now if anyone does not have the Spirit of Christ, he is not His. 10 And if Christ is in you, the body is dead because of sin, but the Spirit is life because of righteousness.

Ephesians 1:13-14—13 In Him you also trusted, after you heard the word of truth, the gospel of your salvation; in whom also, having believed, you were sealed with the Holy Spirit of promise, 14 who is the guarantee of our inheritance until the redemption of the purchased possession, to the praise of His glory.

OBJECTIONS & RESPONSES

See "Simplicity," "Trinity," and "Unity."

PRACTICAL POINTS TO PONDER

1. The Holy Spirit of God lives *within* Believers, and can be *upon* unbelievers.
2. The Holy Spirit of God teaches, guides, comforts, fills, and empowers Believers.
3. The Holy Spirit of God is the seal upon, and within, the Believer that guarantees God's promise of an uncorruptible redemption body.

ECCLESIOLOGY

DEFINITION

Ecclesiology is the study of the church.

DESCRIPTION

The Church is not merely a socio-cultural organization that one can "*join* in." One *becomes* the Church because one is "*born again.*" The Church is the group of people who believe that Jesus Christ is the Son of God, and in so believing, have everlasting life. It is the "Bride of Christ" for which He died, the same for which He will one day return. It is that which was built upon the foundation of the Prophets and the Apostles, with Jesus Christ being the Chief Cornerstone. The Church is the Royal Priesthood and Holy Nation that serves as God's instrumental and vicarious agent upon the Earth to sing His praises while calling people out of the darkness and into His marvelous, moral, saving light.

The Church is the representation of God's Kingdom on Earth. It is comprised of those who, by faith in Jesus Christ, hold dual citizenship: earthly and heavenly. The Church serves as salt (preserves), light (illuminates), and cities set upon a hill (desired destinations seen from afar). Its members—of the One Body of Christ and members of one another—are ambassadors who represent the culture, rule, authority, majesty, and power of God's celestial kingdom while living in this current age of Christ within this earthly, terrestrial realm.

The Church is a spiritual family, united together by like precious faith in Jesus Christ. Its members are the beneficiaries of a blood bond in Christ Jesus, i.e., the blood He shed at Calvary for the remission and forgiveness of sin. It is the keeper, proclaimer, and arbiter of the Gospel, which was entrusted to it once and for all.

The primary goal of the Church is love: to love God with all of its being, and to love others as it loves itself. The Church should give itself to God in worship, praise, and service. To learn, live, and give the Word of God, especially the Gospel of Jesus Christ, while being fully dedicated to God, is the synoptic sum of its existence.

ARGUMENTS

If saved by grace through faith, then the Church.
Saved by grace through faith.
Therefore, the Church.

If you go to Church, then it is true that you are the Church.
However, Church is not what one *does*; Church is what one *is*, by grace through faith in Jesus Christ. In the absence of exercising saving faith in Christ, one cannot be the Church.
Therefore, it is false that you are the Church just because you go to Church.

The Church is the Body of Believers.
The Body of Believers is the Bride of Christ.
The Bride of Christ is the object of Christ's affection.
The object of Christ's affection will one day receive perfection: rescue from this corrupt world via the fulfilled promise of a redemption body for its members.
Thus, the Church will one day be saved from this corrupt world and its members each receive its redemption body.

SCRIPTURES

Matthew 16:18—And I also say to you that you are Peter, and on this rock I will build My church, and the gates of Hades shall not prevail against it.

Matthew 5:13-16—13 "You are the salt of the earth; but if the salt loses its flavor, how shall it be seasoned? It is then good for nothing but to be thrown out and trampled underfoot by men. 14 "You are the light of the world. A city that is set on a hill cannot be hidden. 15 Nor do they light a lamp and put it under a basket, but on a lampstand, and it gives light to all who are in the house. 16 Let your light so shine before men, that they may see your good works and glorify your Father in heaven.

Ephesians 5:25-27—25 Husbands, love your wives, just as Christ also loved the church and gave Himself for her, 26 that He might sanctify and cleanse her with the washing of water by the word, 27 that He might present her to Himself a glorious church, not having spot or wrinkle or any such thing, but that she should be holy and without blemish.

2 Corinthians 5:17-20—17 Therefore, if anyone is in Christ, he is a new creation; old things have passed away; behold, all things have become new. 18 Now all things are of God, who has reconciled us to Himself through Jesus Christ, and has given us the ministry of reconciliation, 19 that is, that God was in Christ reconciling the world to Himself, not imputing their trespasses to them, and has committed to us the word of reconciliation. 20 Now then, we are ambassadors for Christ, as though God were pleading through us: we implore you on Christ's behalf, be reconciled to God.

1 Peter 2:9-10—9 But you are a chosen generation, a royal priesthood, a holy nation, His own special people, that you may proclaim the praises of Him who called you out of darkness into His marvelous light; 10 who once were not a people but are now the people of God, who had not obtained mercy but now have obtained mercy.

OBJECTIONS & RESPONSES

None noted. See also the above arguments in this section.

PRACTICAL POINTS TO PONDER
1. The Church is God's beloved representative on Earth.
2. The Church is God's special purchased possession.
3. The Church will receive the promise of Christ's return for it, and the fulfillment of an incorruptible, eternal body.

ANGELOLOGY

DEFINITION

Angelology is the study of angels.

DESCRIPTION

Angels are spirit beings created by God. They have a beginning in time, but have no end. Angels are non-corporeal, non-physical, spirit beings. The Holy Scriptures do not reveal angels as human beings who died, went to Heaven, received wings, halos, white gowns, and harps. They are presented as beings who were created by, and live to serve the will of, God.

Although angels are immaterial and have no physical bodies, it is clear from Scripture that they are able to actualize some sort of presence. They often appeared to human beings (e.g., Genesis 16, 22, Numbers 22, Judges 6, Luke 2, Acts 5, 7) and have even been said to have been unknowingly entertained by people (Hebrews 13:2).

Angels are free-willed moral agents. When their wills were tested, angels chose to be subject to the will of God. Since angels have no end and are immaterial, they are no longer subject to ontological change. After testing and freely choosing God, their wills are forever subject to the will of God.

Angels are messengers. They helped to reveal the will of God to humankind. One example of this is with Gabriel, who spoke to Daniel (Daniel 8:16, 9:21) and the virgin Mary (Luke 1:19, 26). Angels also appear to have rankings. Michael is called the "Chief Angel" in

Daniel 12. In addition, angels serve in the capacity of protecting and ministering to the needs of humans, per God's plan and purpose.

Per the Scriptures, there are at least two kinds of angels: seraphim and cherubim. Seraphim are a worshipful warrior class of angels that apparently have a guardian presence in the temple of God (e.g., Isaiah 6). Cherubim appear to be multifaceted / multifunctional beings who serve God in various capacities, from guarding the entrance to the Garden of Eden (Genesis 3:24) to figuratively bearing forth the Lord in flight (2 Samuel 22:11, Psalm 18:10).

In essence, angels live to serve God and act according to His will.

ARGUMENTS

The Bible says that Jesus created all things, both seen and unseen.
Angels are (often) unseen beings.
Therefore, angels are created by Jesus.

Angels serve the will of God.
The will of God is to protect those He loves.
Therefore, angels protect those who God loves.

Angels exercised free will to choose among real options.
One option was to serve God or oppose God.
Angels did not choose to oppose God.
Therefore, angels freely chose to serve God.

SCRIPTURES

Genesis 3:22-24—22 Then the Lord God said, "Behold, the man has become like one of Us, to know good and evil. And now, lest he put out his hand and take also of the tree of life, and eat, and live forever"—23 therefore the Lord God sent him out of the garden of

Eden to till the ground from which he was taken. 24 So He drove out the man; and He placed cherubim at the east of the garden of Eden, and a flaming sword which turned every way, to guard the way to the tree of life.

Psalm 104:1-4—Bless the Lord, O my soul! O Lord my God, You are very great: You are clothed with honor and majesty, 2 Who cover Yourself with light as with a garment, Who stretch out the heavens like a curtain. 3 He lays the beams of His upper chambers in the waters, Who makes the clouds His chariot, Who walks on the wings of the wind, 4 Who makes His angels spirits, His ministers a flame of fire.

Isaiah 6:1-3—In the year that King Uzziah died, I saw the Lord sitting on a throne, high and lifted up, and the train of His robe filled the temple. 2 Above it stood seraphim; each one had six wings: with two he covered his face, with two he covered his feet, and with two he flew. 3 And one cried to another and said: "Holy, holy, holy is the Lord of hosts; The whole earth is full of His glory!"

Mark 1:12-13—12 Immediately the Spirit drove Him into the wilderness. 13 And He was there in the wilderness forty days, tempted by Satan, and was with the wild beasts; and the angels ministered to Him.

Hebrews 1:14—Are they not all ministering spirits sent forth to minister for those who will inherit salvation?

OBJECTIONS & RESPONSES

None noted. See also the above arguments in this section.

PRACTICAL POINTS TO PONDER

1. Angels are God-created spirit beings, not human beings who are transformed into angels in Heaven.
2. Angels are servants of God who live to do His will.
3. The will of God is for all to come to repentance. Angels serve as God's protectors for those who will one day be saved.

DEMONOLGY

DEFINITION

Christian Demonology is the study of demons from a Christian perspective.

DESCRIPTION

Demons are spirit beings created by God. They have a beginning in time, but have no end. Demons are non-corporeal, non-physical, spirit beings. They are presented in the Bible as beings who live to defy the will of God and destroy humans.

Demons are free-willed moral agents; they were morally untested angels, in fact. When their wills were tested, demons chose to not be subject to the will of God. Since demons have no end and are immaterial, they are no longer subject to natural change. After testing and freely choosing against God, their wills are forever subject to disobey the will of God. Their nature is deception, falsity (John 8:42-44), and the denigration of those bearing the image of God, i.e., human beings.

Demons are also called "devils." However, the chief of the demons is called "The Devil," or "Satan," the latter meaning "adversary." Demons are limited in knowledge. Satan has greater knowledge than the other devils, yet seemed to have not known that Jesus was really the Christ (Matthew 4:1-11). Demons at least came unto the knowledge that Jesus is the Christ, who also wields the power to destroy them (Mark 1:24, Luke 4:34).

Unlike angels, demons apparently cannot actualize their non-corporeal being in space-time. However, demons are able to possess both (unsaved) human and non-human beings, but they may need permission from God for the latter (e.g., Matthew 8:30-32). Demons can apparently oppress and attack human beings, including Believers (Luke 13:10-15, Acts 19:13-16, 2 Corinthians 12:7-9). However, if one resists, even Satan will flee (James 4:7).

In addition, demons are said to be the actual objects of idol worship by humans. When idols are made, and the people who make them subsequently make offerings to them, they are actually making offerings to demons (Leviticus 17:7, Deuteronomy 32:17, Psalm 106:37, 1 Corinthians 10:20).

Although some demons clearly run amok causing havoc in this world, others are now incarcerated in Hell until the Judgment Day (2 Peter 2:4, Jude 1:6). Demons' final judgment will occur when both Death and Hell are cast into the Lake of Fire (Revelation 20:14).

ARGUMENTS

Demons are created, non-corporeal, immaterial beings.
The nature of demons is to lie, oppose God, and destroy humans.
As immaterial beings, demons are unable to change their nature.
Therefore, the unchanging nature of demons is to lie, oppose God, and destroy humans.

Demons exercised free will to choose among real options.
One option was to serve God or oppose God.
Demons did not choose to serve God.
Therefore, demons freely chose to oppose God.

Demons can only possess unbelievers.
Christians are not unbelievers.
Therefore, demons cannot possess Christians.

SCRIPTURES

Revelation 12:9—So the great dragon was cast out, that serpent of old, called the Devil and Satan, who deceives the whole world; he was cast to the earth, and his angels were cast out with him.

Genesis 3:1-5—3 Now the serpent was more cunning than any beast of the field which the Lord God had made. And he said to the woman, "Has God indeed said, 'You shall not eat of every tree of the garden'?" 2 And the woman said to the serpent, "We may eat the fruit of the trees of the garden; 3 but of the fruit of the tree which is in the midst of the garden, God has said, 'You shall not eat it, nor shall you touch it, lest you die.' " 4 Then the serpent said to the woman, "You will not surely die. 5 For God knows that in the day you eat of it your eyes will be opened, and you will be like God, knowing good and evil."

Job 1:6-7—6 Now there was a day when the sons of God came to present themselves before the Lord, and Satan also came among them. 7 And the Lord said to Satan, "From where do you come?" So Satan answered the Lord and said, "From going to and fro on the earth, and from walking back and forth on it."

1 Peter 5:8—Be sober, be vigilant; because your adversary the devil walks about like a roaring lion, seeking whom he may devour.

Hebrews 2:14-15—14 Inasmuch then as the children have partaken of flesh and blood, He Himself likewise shared in the same, that through death He might destroy him who had the power of death, that is, the devil, 15 and release those who through fear of death were all their lifetime subject to bondage.

Matthew 8:28-29—28 When He had come to the other side, to the country of the Gergesenes, there met Him two demon-possessed men, coming out of the tombs, exceedingly fierce, so that no one could pass that way. 29 And suddenly they cried out, saying, "What have we to do with You, Jesus, You Son of God? Have You come here to torment us before the time?"

OBJECTIONS & RESPONSES
None noted. See also the above arguments in this section.

PRACTICAL POINTS TO PONDER
1. Demons are defeated, fallen angels whose power and knowledge are limited.
2. Demons' nature is to oppose God, lie about anything, possess and / or oppress people, and to generally deceive human beings about the truth of God's love for them.
3. Satan is the leader of the demons, but will flee if resisted.
4. Though now defeated, all demons will one day be destroyed by God in the Great Judgment.

ESCHATOLOGY

DEFINITION

Eschatology is the study of the end times.

DESCRIPTION

Eschatology is derived from the Greek word *eschatos* (es'-khat-os), meaning "last," "farthest," or "final." The Bible has several promises and predictive prophecies regarding future events about God's plan and purpose for humanity. They are primarily about God's righteous judgment of free moral agents, i.e., distributing to each one the reward or punishment that each one deserves. Some of the prophecies were fulfilled in a contemporary sense, yet with future implications (e.g., Isaiah 7:4), while others were later fulfilled (e.g., Isaiah 53), and yet others apparently remain unfulfilled (e.g., Daniel 12, Matthew 24, Revelation 4-22).

How these promises and prophecies about end-time events have unfolded, or will unfold, has been a subject of great and intense debate throughout the history of humankind, even unto this day. The vast majority of the disputes revolve around the science of biblical interpretation, also called *hermeneutics*.

Those who employ a *historical-grammatical* approach, taking into consideration things like the types of genres, syntax, and grammar, may view certain eschatological passages as not having occurred in human history, but will occur in the future. Others who may use an *allegorical* or *spiritual* approach could view the events as occurring now, either in an actual real sense, or in a spiritual sense. Still others believe that the events are not likely to, or will not, occur at all.

Much of the eschatological debate revolves around the timing of the Church's Rapture: 1) before, during, or after the *Tribulation* period of God's judgment of humankind, and 2) before, during, or after Christ's *Millennial Reign* on Earth. There is one view, called the *Preterist* view, that says there will be no rapture, and this view will be briefly presented below.

Nevertheless, the vast majority of Believers expect that one day 1) Jesus will Rapture the Church, 2) God will judge the world, 3) the heavens and earth will both be destroyed and renewed, and 4) the Church will be with God in unified, loving peace forever. As stated above, the order of these events, and how the Scriptures describe them, are subject to debate.

Even so, there are at least seven different eschatological views. The table below summarizes each position. The way it is read is that as an "x" intersects a column and row, it would be read "row/column." Thus, for "Pre-Millennial Reign of Christ" intersecting with "Pre-Trib Rapture," it would be "Pre-Mil / Pre-Trib," meaning that the Church will be raptured before the Tribulation Period and the Millennial Reign of Christ.

NOTE: the *Amillennial* view says that there will be no Millennial kingdom; there will be the end of the seven-year tribulation, followed by the rapture of the church, the end of this current age, and the beginning of the new eternal age. The *Preterist* view denies both the Millennial Kingdom and the Rapture; all prophecies have been fulfilled in Christ's coming, and the world will one day simply be "Christianized" and live in peace.

Table of Abridged Eschatalogical Views

	Pre-Trib Rapture	Mid-Trib Rapture	Post-Trib Rapture
Pre-Millennial Reign of Christ	X	X	X
Post-Millennial Reign of Christ	N/A	N/A	X

Finally, despite many claims to the contrary by many people through the millennia, no one knows the day nor the hour when Christ will return (Matthew 24:36). There are "warning signs" of His coming (Matthew 24:3-8), but that day will not come until God's appointed time, and no one will be aware of its actual coming until then (2 Peter 3:10). God is indeed merciful and does not wish that any should perish, but that all would come to repentance (2 Peter 3:9). Thus, we should rejoice that His Love has allayed Wrath from having already been poured out upon humankind.

ARGUMENTS

If there was a beginning of the world, there will be an end of the world.
There was a beginning of the world.
Thus, there will be an end of the world.

Jesus promised to return for the Church.
Jesus always keeps His promises.
Therefore, Jesus will return for the Church.

God promised to one day judge the world in righteousness.
Righteousness is Justice.
Justice gives each one what is due: good for good, and bad for bad.
Thus, God will one day give each one what each one is due.

SCRIPTURES

Daniel 12:4, 9—4 "But you, Daniel, shut up the words, and seal the book until the time of the end; many shall run to and fro, and knowledge shall increase." 9 And he said, "Go your way, Daniel, for the words are closed up and sealed till the time of the end."

Matthew 24:4-8—4 And Jesus answered and said to them: "Take heed that no one deceives you. 5 For many will come in My name, saying, 'I am the Christ,' and will deceive many. 6 And you will hear of wars and rumors of wars. See that you are not troubled; for all these things must come to pass, but the end is not yet. 7 For nation will rise against nation, and kingdom against kingdom. And there will be famines, pestilences, and earthquakes in various places. 8 All these are the beginning of sorrows."

Matthew 24:36—"But of that day and hour no one knows, not even the angels of heaven, but My Father only."

2 Peter 3:10-12—10 But the day of the Lord will come as a thief in the night, in which the heavens will pass away with a great noise, and the elements will melt with fervent heat; both the earth and the works that are in it will be burned up. 11 Therefore, since all these things will be dissolved, what manner of persons ought you to be in holy conduct and godliness, 12 looking for and hastening the coming of the day of God, because of which the heavens will be dissolved, being on fire, and the elements will melt with fervent heat?

Eschatology

1 Corinthians 15:50-52— 50 Now this I say, brethren, that flesh and blood cannot inherit the kingdom of God; nor does corruption inherit incorruption. 51 Behold, I tell you a mystery: We shall not all sleep, but we shall all be changed—52 in a moment, in the twinkling of an eye, at the last trumpet. For the trumpet will sound, and the dead will be raised incorruptible, and we shall be changed.

1 Thessalonians 4:16-18—16 For the Lord Himself will descend from heaven with a shout, with the voice of an archangel, and with the trumpet of God. And the dead in Christ will rise first. 17 Then we who are alive and remain shall be caught up together with them in the clouds to meet the Lord in the air. And thus we shall always be with the Lord. 18 Therefore comfort one another with these words.

Revelation 20:4-6—4 And I saw thrones, and they sat on them, and judgment was committed to them. Then I saw the souls of those who had been beheaded for their witness to Jesus and for the word of God, who had not worshiped the beast or his image, and had not received his mark on their foreheads or on their hands. And they lived and reigned with Christ for a thousand years. 5 But the rest of the dead did not live again until the thousand years were finished. This is the first resurrection. 6 Blessed and holy is he who has part in the first resurrection. Over such the second death has no power, but they shall be priests of God and of Christ, and shall reign with Him a thousand years.

Revelation 20:11-15—11 Then I saw a great white throne and Him who sat on it, from whose face the earth and the heaven fled away. And there was found no place for them. 12 And I saw the dead, small and great, standing before God, and books were opened. And another book was opened, which is the Book of Life. And the dead were judged according to their works, by the things which were written in the books. 13 The sea gave up the dead who were in it, and Death and Hades delivered up the dead who were in them. And they were judged, each one according to his works. 14 Then Death and Hades were cast into the lake of fire. This is the second death. 15 And anyone not found written in the Book of Life was cast into the lake of fire.

Revelation 21:1-5—Now I saw a new heaven and a new earth, for the first heaven and the first earth had passed away. Also there was no more sea. 2 Then I, John, saw the holy city, New Jerusalem, coming down out of heaven from God, prepared as a bride adorned for her husband. 3 And I heard a loud voice from heaven saying, "Behold, the tabernacle of God is with men, and He will dwell with them, and they shall be His people. God Himself will be with them and be their God. 4 And God will wipe away every tear from their eyes; there shall be no more death, nor sorrow, nor crying. There shall be no more pain, for the former things have passed away." 5 Then He who sat on the throne said, "Behold, I make all things new." And He said to me, "Write, for these words are true and faithful."

OBJECTIONS & RESPONSES

See "Omniscience" re: Jesus' knowledge of the end times. Also consider "Love," "Justice," "Mercy," "Truth," "Hamartiology," and "Soteriology."

PRACTICAL POINTS TO PONDER

1. God will one day condemn all evil and wickedness in this world.
2. No one knows the day or time that God has appointed for these events.
3. As long as there is "today," God's Mercy allows any person to accept His gift of Grace: salvation through faith in Jesus Christ.

ACKNOWLEDGEMENTS

ACKNOWLEDGEMENTS

Aquinas, Thomas. *Summa Theologica*. Benziger Bros. edition, translated by the Fathers of the English Dominican Province, 1947.

Bloesch, Donald G. *Essentials of Evangelical Theology, Vol. 1*. Peabody, MA: Prince Press, 1998.

Geisler, Norman L. and Ronald M. Brooks. *Come Let Us Reason*. Grand Rapids: Random House, 1996.

Geisler, Norman L. *Systematic Theology, Vol. 2*. Bloomington, MN: Bethany House Publishers, 2003.

_____. *Systematic Theology, Vol. 3*. Bloomington, MN: Bethany House Publishers, 2003.

_____. *Systematic Theology, Vol. 4*. Bloomington, MN: Bethany House Publishers, 2003.

Hodge, Charles. *Systematic Theology, Vol. 1*. Hendrickson Publishers, Inc., 1999.

Lightner, Robert. *The Last Days Handbook, revised and updated*. Nashville: Thomas Nelson Publishers, 1997.

Nagel, Thomas. *Mind and Cosmos. Why the Materialist Neo-Darwinian Conception of Nature Is Almost Certainly False*. New York: Oxford University Press. 2012.

Zuck, Roy B. *Basic Bible Interpretation: A Practical Guide to Discovering Biblical Truth*. Colorado Springs, CO USA and Paris, Ontario CAN: Cook Communications Ministries; Eastbourne, England: Kingsway Communications, LTD, 1991.

www.ingramcontent.com/pod-product-compliance
Lightning Source LLC
Chambersburg PA
CBHW071116160426
43196CB00013B/2582